Prepress for Digital Printing

An introduction to prepress methods for the digital age

John C. Clem and Wade J. Link

Edited and Foreword by Peter I. Muir

Trio Publications/Baldwin, KS

Paperback Edition
First Edition - 2003

Library of Congress Catalog Card Number: 20-03094843

ISBN 0-9678620-0-9

Authors: John C. Clem and Wade J. Link
Title: Prepress for Digital Printing:
An introduction to prepress methods for the digital age

Edition: 1st edition
Includes Index

Printed in the United States

Right of use for some reference materials utilized in the creation of this book were granted by Peter I. Muir of I.O. Technologies. The additional use of these materials by other parties is not permitted under this agreement.

The cover and body of this book printed with a Xerox DocuColor iGen3 Digital Production Press.

Published by:
Trio Publications
102 Sante Fe
Baldwin, KS 66006

Disclaimer

This document has been created as a basic guide to preparing digital files (books, pamphlets, brochures, etc...) for printing/publishing utilizing digital printing equipment. Although the authors and publisher have exhaustively researched the subjects covered within this document to ensure completeness and accuracy and all information within, this document is assumed correct, but may contain typographical errors, informational errors, inaccuracies, or omissions. Neither the authors, nor any persons and or companies associated with this publication accept responsibility nor liability for personal injury, property damage, or any other loss or damages arising from actions inspired by this book. Nor shall the authors or publisher be liable for any loss of profit or any other commercial damages, including but not limited to special, incidental, consequential, or other damages. It is entirely the responsibility of any person or persons using this document to understand and properly use said information. Any slights against companies, corporations, products, organizations, or people within this document are unintentional. If you do not wish to be bound by the above, you may return this book to the publisher for full refund. Refund qualification based on the requirement that the returned book is in re-salable condition, and is subject to the publisher's discretion, and the original sales receipt must accompany the book. Refund not to include sales tax or shipping costs.

There are many references to companies and their products throughout this book. It would be impractical to designate each instance of reference with the use of a copyright, trademark or registered trademark symbol. A list of product names and manufacturer names protected by these laws is included in the appendix.

Prepress for Digital Printing

An introduction to prepress methods for the digital age

John C. Clem and Wade J. Link

Edited and Foreword by Peter I. Muir

Trio Publications/Baldwin, KS

Table of Contents

Foreword

How digital is your life?

Not a day goes by that each and every one of us isn't touched or influenced by digital devices. I recently asked some of my students to list all things digital they come in contact with directly, or indirectly, in a 24 hour period and here is what they came up with:

PDAs, cell phones, personal computers, planes, trains, automobiles, children's toys, environmental controls, stereos, printers, dishwashers, car washes, clocks, cameras, scanners, ATMs, keycards, gym equipment, phones, TVs, faxes, blinking sneakers, pagers, toilets, sinks, robots, watches, GPS systems, alarms, hearing aids, pacemakers, MRI machines, sprinklers, the Internet, surgical instruments, and on and on and on.

How many more can you think of? The list above took only 2 minutes before I thought I had enough to make my point...they were ready to keep going!

All things digital surround our lives! We would have a hard time in 2003 trying to go through a day without using something digital. All this digital technology and even more to come; keeping up with it is hard to do. As older digital systems are being replaced by newer digital systems, we are constantly being educated on what's new, how to best use it and avoid breaking it.

I was recently asked, “Did digital grow up around you or did you grow up around digital?” I stopped and thought for a long minute about such a great question. I am probably the last generation who can say digital grew up around me, because if you look at the 20 somethings today, they grew up around digital. If you doubt this, go to their schools and you will see computers not only in the classroom, but also in their book bags! They've got cell phones, pagers, MP3 players, video games, digital cameras and printers as well.

For those of us who digital grew up around, we have to make a choice, will I fight it or accept it? My company is in the business of helping people utilize technology through education. As a result of learning about technology and how to use it, people realize they can make money, make their lives easier and make themselves look good.

The last fifteen years have been lots of fun. If you weren't paying attention in the late 80's you may have missed the development of three small digital technologies: the Apple Macintosh, Aldus PageMaker and Adobe PostScript. Today you use personal computers made by Apple and others. You use software to layout “pages” for print and the Internet. These three small technologies started a revolution. During a time when the art and craftsmanship of printing was completed by highly skilled labor, these technologies were seen as mere blips on the horizon soon to go away-we didn't need to worry. Those people who chose not to worry about it have either embraced the digital technology or moved onto another occupation or retired.

Not long ago, if you wanted something printed you went to see a person called a printer. Today we simply press a button on our screen and presto-a printer on our desk, on the floor, down the hall, downstairs or across town starts printing-voila! You are a printer!

There are more and more people using digital means to communicate everyday. As people get involved who have never done it before, we run into problems. Problems that cost us money, take up our time and potentially influence the quality of our work.

When it comes down to digital printing we need to design our work with the end use in mind. Instead of filling the white screen with information, step back and do some old fashioned planning before we grab these new tools and start designing.

John Clem and Wade Link have put together one of the most useful introductions to the designing and preparation of digital files for digital printing. Whether you are someone who designs printed pieces or provides a service by printing other peoples files, or you do both, you will find a lot of useful information to help you.

Digital printing (using inkjet and toner based print technology) has firmly established itself as a viable market. As we embrace the market and take advantage of the technology we should take the time to learn about how this new way of communicating can not only change the way we communicate but also change the way we create files for print.

Take the time to learn about the new technologies being developed around you. Your life is more digital than you think and by taking the time to learn more about it, the easier your life will become.

Peter Muir
President
I.O. Technologies

John Clem is a Customer Support Analyst on the DocuColor iGen3 Digital Production Press launch team. He has been with Xerox for 6 years supporting printing industry clients and workflows. John is a self-published author, has a BS in Marketing and a Masters degree in Management Information Systems. John may be contacted at john.clem@usa.xerox.com.

Wade Link is a SmartPress Production Consultant assigned to the DocuColor iGen3 Digital Production Press launch team. Wade has worked in the printing industry for more than 20 years as a graphic designer, art director, and advertising agency owner. Wade is an expert in prepress, applications, and printing technologies. Wade may be contacted at wade.link@usa.xerox.com.

Peter Muir is president of I.O. Technologies, a graphic communication education, consulting, and research company. Peter has been deeply committed to education and technology since his first experiences with the Apple Macintosh in 1984. He is the author of the Preflight Pocket Primer and speaks regularly at trade events such as GraphExpo, Seybold and Print on productivity, profitability and partnership topics. He also has an MS in Printing Technology from RIT. Peter may be contacted at pmuir@iotechnologies.ws.

Introduction

An old Chinese proverb states, "May you live in interesting times." In the printing industry, these are certainly interesting times. Advances in computer technology has radically changed the printing industry in the past 5 years; this trend will only continue in the future. Also, clients are demanding more color work, have more complex jobs, require shorter print runs, want more services, and need faster turnaround times.

One of the most important recent technical developments has been the introduction of very high quality digital printing equipment.

Digital printing equipment differs from traditional offset lithography printing in that it uses an electronic means of creating a printed image as opposed to using printing plates. Examples of digital printing devices include your desktop laser printer, inkjet printer, office printer, or high-speed digital press.

Digital output may also have a slightly different appearance than offset printed materials. Some people may see a difference, some may think they do. Some people will see no difference and most importantly, more people are finding it acceptable—or don't care about the differences!

Digital printing is not the best option for all printing requirements. It is not a replacement for offset printing, it is a complement to it. Digital printing can complement traditional printing technologies by providing an economical option where offset printers are not cost effective. Examples of this are pre-production samples, additional printing capacity, pre-offset production, post-offset production, etc. Digital printing gives the service provider a production option that was not available in the past, bringing more jobs and more money into their business.

Digital printing lends itself very well to cost effective short-run print jobs, proofs, posters, one-off samples, book covers, print jobs requiring fast turnaround times, and print jobs with personalized (variable) data requirements.

Since the printed image created by a digital printer requires less setup for production than traditional printing methods, it is typically more economical (less cost per impression) for use in short-run printing situations. When printing larger quantities, digital printing may or may not be the most economical solution; your service provider can give you information regarding the most economical printing method for your job.

Also, by utilizing print-on-demand capabilities for your materials, digital printing technologies help to reduce quantities of printed materials, reducing your cash outlay for those materials, also reducing warehousing costs, transportation costs, unused materials, damaged materials, and potential waste.

For printing documents with variable information, digital printing is generally the best solution. In a variable data application a digital printer can create the body of the document as well as the variable customer data in a single pass. This can be accomplished for print runs of 1 to 10,000,000 at the same cost per impression. If you are changing the data on each page, traditional printing methods will never be as cost effective.

Digital printing is a rapidly changing and evolving technology. It is important that you keep abreast of these changes in order to remain a valuable resource within the graphics industry. Additional information can be garnered from current digital printing users, user groups, manufacturers, and service providers who have embraced this relatively new technology.

How to Use this Book

This document was created to provide information regarding digital file preparation to a wide audience of varying skill levels; graphic designers, service providers, and equipment operators. It is intended as a basic guide and reference. Because the scope of this information is so broad, not all sections will be relevant to everyone. You may find it useful to read the entire document, only lookup items of interest in specific chapters or perhaps a mix of both.

We know that not everyone will agree with the information provided in this book. This information is simply the opinion of the authors and the editor. If you think we really missed a big issue or have included incorrect information, send your thoughts to john.clem@usa.xerox.com.

The term printer, printing press, and press are all used in this document to describe some type of digital printing device. Any reference to an offset lithographic printing press will always include the word "offset". The company or organization providing the printing service will always be referred to as the service provider.

The key points of each section are summarized at the end of the section under "Keep this in mind."

The index and glossary may also help identify the location of specific topics and to define terms. Glossary terms are indicated by italic text. There is also and expanded glossary of printing terminology available at: www.coloroutput.com/glossary.

Additional information can be obtained from the Internet addresses and books listed in the appendix.

We acknowledge that information in printed form is locked and cannot be updated as the industry changes. But, since this book is being printed exclusively using digital printing equipment, we can update the information in it more frequently and keep the material more current. We will also post the most up-to-date information on our web site, www.coloroutput.com. Keep your eye on it.

1

First Things First

- Good Preparation
- Color Perception
- Your Service Provider
- Structuring Your Files for Submission
- New Application Features

First Things First

This book was created in the hope of providing you with key points of information to help you create better electronic files and designs, giving you better results when printing to digital printing equipment. The material in this book is intended to highlight issues that are specifically important to digital printing equipment.

Good Preparation

Today, virtually all printed materials involve the use of computers in the creation of artwork and in the printing process. How you manage your digital files is very important to successful output. You, as the content creator, are responsible for understanding the systems you are using and for properly preparing your files. A little effort on your part to better understand this process will greatly improve the quality of your work. If you are unsure of something regarding file preparation, ask your service provider, they are generally very knowledgeable about the capabilities of their equipment.
In the prepress process, there are a number of rules that are accepted and followed. The majority of these rules date from the beginnings of computerized prepress when computers were not very powerful. Computers today are much more powerful and therefore more capable. This capability allows you to bend many of these traditional digital prepress rules with no ill effects. Bending these rules can allow you to work and design more efficiently and faster. However, bending some rules may still get you into trouble. We will try to give you an idea of what rules you can bend as well as those you should not.

Color Perception

Everyone's eyes are different and we all see colors differently. We can see colors because of the cone shaped cells in the retinas of our eyes, which are sensitive to either the red, green, or blue wavelengths of light. The distribution of these cells varies from person to person. Because of these differences, we all see or perceive any given color a little differently than anyone else. These differences in color perception also affect how we perceive colors in printed materials.

The light that illuminates or reflects off an object also affects the colors we see. All light sources have a color bias to some degree, blue, yellow, or red. Most of the time we see colors as a result of light bouncing off of an object (an exception is a computer monitor). The color of the light bouncing off an object affects how we see or perceive the color of that object. Also, the color of an object adjacent to what we are viewing can also affect the colors we see.

Because the color bias of the light used to view an object will affect the colors we perceive, it is important we use a controlled light source for evaluating printed materials. The varying sources

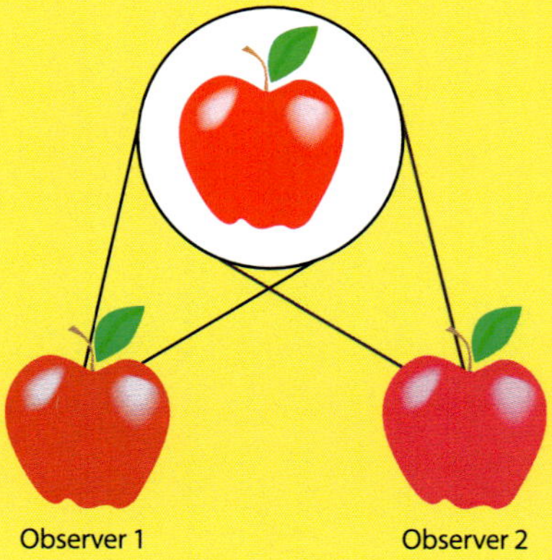

Different people see the same object differently

Adjacency Affect

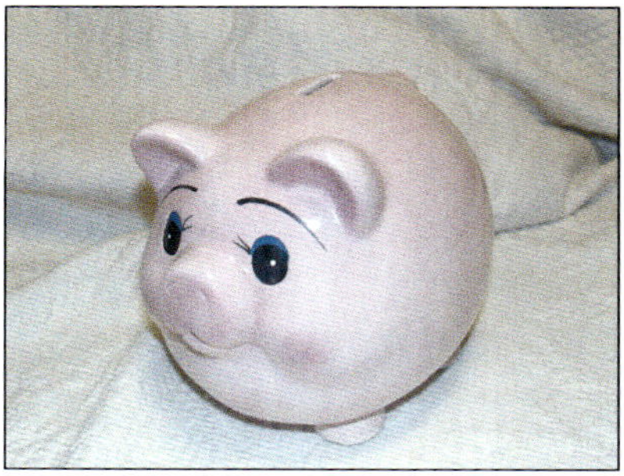

Daylight

Florescent

Incandescent

The color bias of the light source affects the colors we perceive

of lighting in our work environments (incandescent, fluorescent, sodium vapor, sunlight etc.) all have a differing color bias. Light booths with known lighting characteristics are used in the printing industry for evaluating and approving printed color materials. The color of a light source is defined in degrees Kelvin. Two common options are the D50 (5000 Degrees Kelvin) and the D65 (6500 Degrees Kelvin or daylight) lighting standards. If you choose to evaluate color, be sure to remember the light source you are using will affect the resulting color you perceive.

There are different technologies available for color printing. Some of these methods use water based inks, some use solvent based inks, while others such as xerography use plastic toners.

All of these different technologies will produce final output that will appear different in varying degrees. The paper or media that is used will also affect the final output. Creating media that will match across multiple platforms and technologies (four-color press, digital press, web/internet) requires knowledge, patience, time, and money.

Structuring your files for submission

Digital files created on a computer typically consist of multiple files that will all have to be sent to your service provider for output. An exception to this is the use of a PDF workflow (see chapter 7 for more details). These various files consist of the main application file, any graphics or image files, and the fonts used in the creation of the design. It is important that you are thorough and consistent in how you package your files for submission to the service provider. Submitting your files properly will greatly reduce problems for both of you.

The generally accepted method for submitting source files is to package them into three folders: layout, graphics, and fonts. In these folders you place the appropriate files, the native application file in the layout folder, all graphics in the graphics folder, and all fonts in the fonts folder.

Most layout applications have a feature that will help you identify and collect these files. Some work better than others, test them and use it!

Leaving out any graphics or *fonts* may cause a delay in the output of your file so be thorough.

The exception to this rule is the use of *PDFs* for file submission, and many

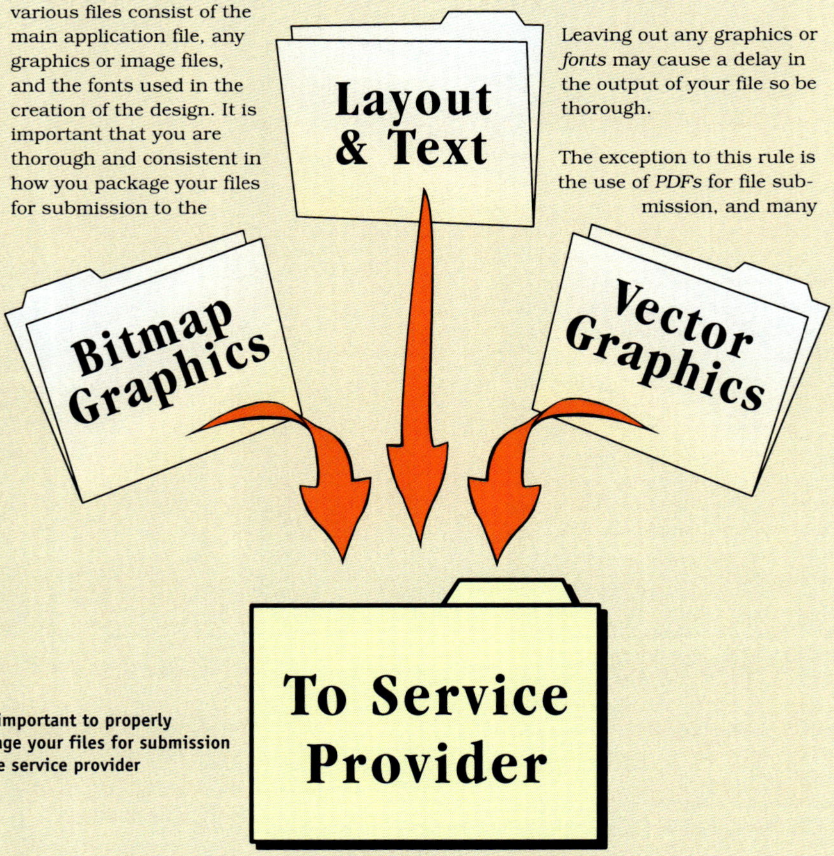

It is important to properly package your files for submission to the service provider

service providers are encouraging their use. If they are created properly, they greatly simplify file management for the service provider. The downside is a limitation to the file corrections that can be made by the service provider. Confirm the preferred method before submitting your files.

Also, at minimum provide a black and white laser or inkjet proof of your design, a color proof is better. This proof gives the service provider something to compare with the final output. It is the only way they can be sure your graphics and photos are printing properly, images are in their right places, *fonts* have printed correctly, and text has not reflowed.

Keep these things in mind when creating your designs, dealing with your customers and your service provider. Doing so will make your job much easier and more enjoyable.

Your Service Provider

When in doubt, ask your service provider. Your service provider is in the business of printing for profit or to provide a service. Because this is their business, they are generally very knowledgeable about their equipment, its capabilities, application issues, and preferred file formats. Some service providers offer printing guides to their customers containing information about proper file preparation specifically for their shop and equipment.

If you have questions about anything related to the printing equipment used to create your job or any issues regarding the applications you will be using, be sure to ask your service provider. It is in their best interest to give you good information. Fewer problems printing your job result in faster job turn around.

"When in doubt, ask your service provider. Your service provider is in the business of printing for profit. Because this is their business, they are generally very knowledgeable about their equipment, its capabilities, application issues, and preferred file formats."

New Application Features

Other things to be aware of are new applications and features. Because technology is advancing so quickly and computers are becoming so powerful, many new features are being added to existing applications. Most of these features can aid productivity and promote creativity, but some can also cause you trouble. Before using some cool new feature in your design, think of how this might impact production. Will a RIP support it? Will it greatly increase processing time?

The same goes for new applications. Before using a new application, check to see if your service provider can support it. Also, consider how you are using the application. Will sending a file to the *RIP* containing 30 different layers cause a problem? Chances are it will.

Do your homework and understand the good and the bad, as well as the ugly for your new application or feature.

2

Applications & Files

- Desktop Publishing Applications
- PostScript and other PDLs
- Text & Fonts
- Graphic File Formats
- Other File Issues
- Image Capture

Applications & Files

The results of your final output will depend almost entirely on the way in which the work was created. The better the job you perform in creating your work, the better your final product. Using the correct applications for their intended purposes will yield the best results.

Desktop Publishing Applications

If you plan to print a complex document that includes many graphics and photos, you should use a desktop publishing (DTP) software application for the layout. Examples of these programs are Adobe Illustrator, QuarkXPress, Adobe InDesign, Adobe Pagemaker or Adobe Framemaker. All of these programs are capable of creating high quality output, but they are also more expensive than generic office applications.

There are four basic types of applications used in creating a design: word processing programs, bitmap graphic editing programs, vector graphic editing programs, and page layout programs. You should always use the application for its intended purpose. Even though a word processor may have some of the features of a page layout application, try not to use it as such. You will create additional problems for yourself and your service provider.

Many people use typical office applications for creating printed materials. These applications are not specifically designed to work with complex layouts and may prove troublesome when submitting files to a service provider or printing device.

Regardless of the software used to create your print job, it is important to understand your service provider may, or may not have the application you used to create your work. If your service provider does not have your *DTP* software, they will not be able to work with a raw or native application file. You may need to convert your file into a file type that is more common to the printing industry. This subject will be covered later in the book.

Word processing applications are mainly designed to create and edit text. Examples of word processing software are Microsoft Word or Corel WordPerfect. Try not to use these programs for layout, they don't have the layout features required for this task and may prove difficult to print from.

Bitmap graphic editing applications are designed to manipulate bitmap graphic files created by scanners or digital cameras. Bitmap graphics are comprised of a fixed grid of picture elements (pixels) to form an image (*TIFF* or BMP files for example) and are resolution dependent. These images may become fuzzy or jagged if scaled too large.

Examples of these applications are Adobe Photoshop or Corel Photo Paint (Photoshop is the de facto graphic arts industry standard). These applications should be used to edit or change bitmap graphic files or create original artwork to be placed into other applications, not as a page layout application.

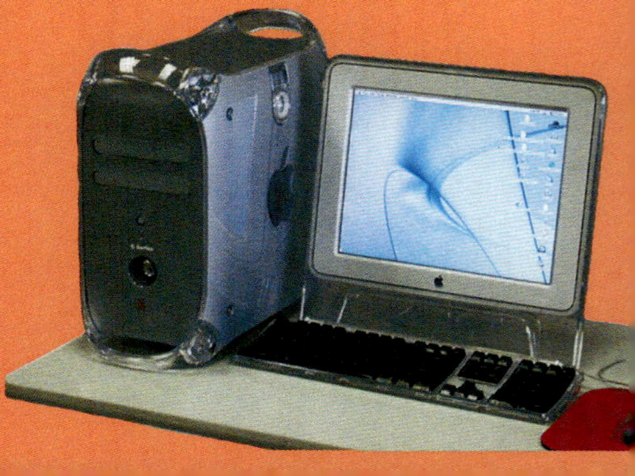

Vector graphic editing programs are designed to create and edit vector-based graphics. Examples of vector graphic programs are Adobe Illustrator, Macromedia Freehand, or Corel Draw. Vector based graphics are created by defining points within an image and mathematically calculating curves that represent lines. Vector based graphics are resolution independent and can be scaled up or down with no loss of quality. These programs should be used to create vector-based graphics to be linked to a page layout application. Certain industries, such as packaging, may use this type of software to create a single page design, this is not recommended for multiple page layouts.

Page layout programs are designed to bring all these elements, text, bitmap graphics and vector graphics together in a manageable way. They can be used to create one page flyers and posters as well as newsletters and books.

Examples of page layout applications are QuarkXPress, Adobe InDesign, and Adobe Pagemaker. These programs are specifically designed to handle components created by other applications and provide you with the image and typography management, and the output options required to suitably print your job.

Your service provider has probably encountered more issues than you have while using these applications. Check with them to see if they have any tips or tricks to help you with your design.

Keep this in mind

1. Each application was designed for a specific purpose. Use it that way.
2. Realize that bending some prepress rules may cause you headaches when you attempt to output your work.

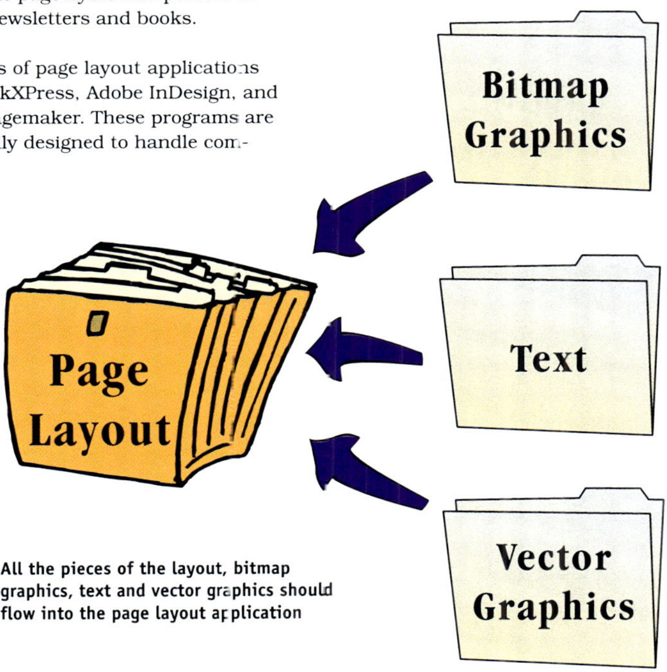

All the pieces of the layout, bitmap graphics, text and vector graphics should flow into the page layout application

PostScript and other PDLs

When you print a document from your computer to a large printing system, your document is most often converted into *PostScript* or some other PDL and then sent to the printing system. *PostScript* is a page description language (PDL) developed by Adobe Systems in the late 1980's to address the issue of defining layout information on a page. *PostScript* defines all the elements on the page: text, pictures, graphics, backgrounds, borders, etc. Since that time, PostScript has become the printing industry standard PDL.

Everything you create in your design can be translated into *PostScript*, both good and bad. If you don't follow standard prepress rules the *PostScript* file you create can be more complex than necessary. This may result in your file failing to process at the printer.

Just Remember:

Good File Preparation =
Good *PostScript* =
Successful Output!!!

The *PostScript* code created by your computer is sent to what is commonly called the *RIP* or *raster image processor.* A *RIP* is also known as a *DFE* or *digital front end.* Every digital printing device: inkjet printers, dye sublimation printers, and laser printing devices has some sort of a *RIP*. But not all digital printing devices can process *PostScript* code because this feature must be licensed from Adobe Systems. Other printing devices may use Hewlett Packard's PCL page description language. Using a different language when printing can easily cause differences in output.

Also, RIPs are scalable depending on the printing technology, smaller RIPs for smaller, slower output devices and larger RIPs for larger, faster and more complex devices. Since *PostScript* is used extensively by the printing industry we will only discuss *PostScript* compliant RIPs in this book.

The *RIP* converts the *PostScript* and all of its instructions into a language that the printing system can understand or machine language. This data is then converted to printed output by whatever printing technology is being utilized.

Text and Fonts

There are two main types of fonts used in DTP. Adobe Type 1 and TrueType fonts are available for Macintosh and Windows based computers. Adobe PostScript Type 1 fonts are more common on Macintosh computers while TrueType fonts are more common on Windows based computers. In the printing industry, Adobe Type 1 fonts

```
%!PS-Adobe-3.0
%%Title: Microsoft Word - xterm.doc
%%Creator: AdobePS5.dll Version 5.2.1
%%CreationDate: 7/30/2002 16:26:23
%%BoundingBox: (atend)
%%Pages: (atend)
%%Orientation: Portrait
%%PageOrder: Ascend
%%DocumentNeededResources: (atend)
%%DocumentSuppliedResources: (atend)
%%DocumentData: Clean7Bit
%%TargetDevice: (Scitex Station) (3011.105)
%%LanguageLevel: 3
%%EndComments

%%BeginDefaults
%%PageBoundingBox: 0 0 612 792
%%ViewingOrientation: 1 0 0 1
%%EndDefaults


%%BeginProlog
%%BeginResource: file Pscript_WinNT_Error
/currentpacking where{pop/oldpack currentpac
setpacking}if}if/$brkpage 64 dict def $brkpag
ne{=string cvs}if dup length 6 mul/tx exch de
def/tox exch def 1 setgray newpath tox toy 2
```

An example of PostScript header code

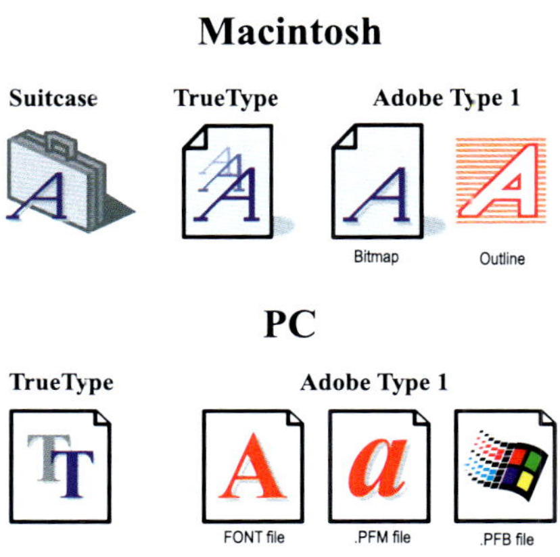

Fonts differ between the Macintosh and Windows platforms

are more common, but TrueType fonts are becoming more acceptable (older RIPs may not be able to process TrueType fonts, and some service providers will not accept files containing TrueType fonts).

There is a newer font structure called Open Type. These *fonts* are designed to be platform independent, allowing them to be used on both Macintosh and Windows computers. Using Open Type *fonts* allows you to easily move files between platforms. There are two issues with Open Type *fonts*: the file size of the *fonts* and *RIP* compatibility. These *fonts* are larger than others because they are platform independent. Their use will make your files larger. Also, some RIPs may not be able to handle them today, check with your service provider to be sure.

Keep this in mind

1. You will get the best results if your service provider uses the same computer platform you used to create the file. There are slight differences between the Adobe Type 1 fonts for Windows and Macintosh systems that can affect the final output.

2. If you are taking an application file to your service provider, you should also include all the fonts used in creating your file. This includes any fonts embedded within EPS (Encapsulated PostScript) graphic files. Adobe Type 1 fonts consist of both a screen font (used for the monitor display) and a printer font (used by the printing equipment); be sure to include both.

3. There are Type 1 and TrueType fonts with the same names, but they may be from different font manufacturers and contain characters that do not match. This is especially troublesome for service providers since they do not know which font you used. You should include a font list that indicates font types, manufacturer, version as well as font names. Never rename a font as this will only cause more problems.

4. Most applications have the ability to make a font bold, italic, or underlining (using the bold, italic, and underline buttons on your tool bar). This is called a locally stylized font. Avoid using this option. These fonts may look fine on your screen, but many high-end rips will strip off your applied styles leaving only the original font that was specified in your document or replace it with the default printer font. If you want a bold font, use a font that has a bold typeface available. Different font families offer true bold and italic fonts. Use these to maintain the integrity of your design.

5. TrueType fonts may reflow when you use a different print driver other than the one used to the create the file. A work around for this is to

Printer font

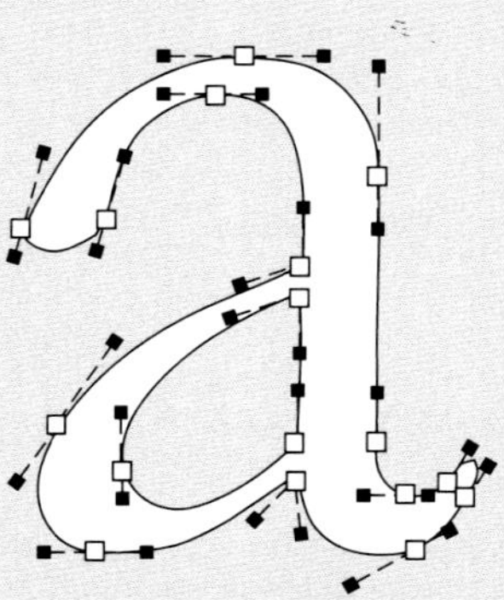

Vector based printer font

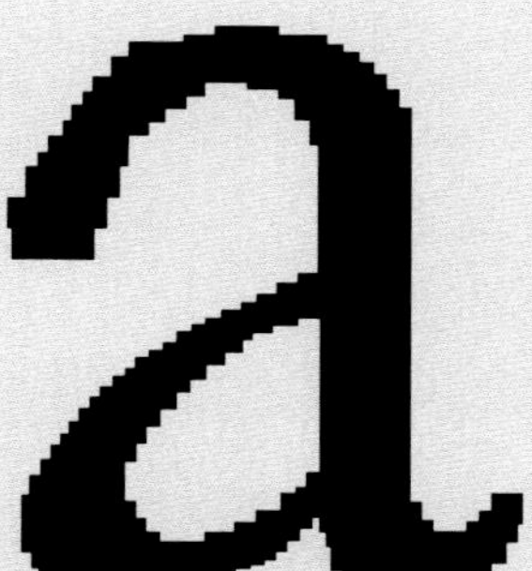

Bitmap screen font

determine what printer will be used to output your files and establish this as your default printer. Then fonts should not reflow when sent to your service provider.

6. You should use only one font type (Type 1, TrueType, etc.) in any file in order to reduce the chance of problems when ripping the file.

7. Remember, all fonts are software licensed for use. Read your font licenses to be sure that your are complying with your license agreement.

8. Lastly, when you package your files for submission to the service provider, create a folder called "Fonts" and place a copy of all the fonts used in your document in that folder.

Graphic File Formats

Graphic file refers to any image, photograph or artwork, utilized in your design. You should be aware of several issues dealing with the file types used, how they are managed, and their relationship with your DTP software.

In general, you will use an application program to manipulate the graphic file (change the size, format, color, shading, etc.), before you link the graphic to your *DTP* software. Examples of these graphic programs are Photoshop, Illustrator, Freehand, and Photo Paint.

There are two basic types of graphic files, *lossless* file types and *lossy* file types. *Lossless* files contain the most information, but will also be quite large. *Lossy* files can be smaller in size, but sacrifice image quality. The *lossless/lossy* description is determined by the *compression* rate of the file type and the resulting image quality. *Lossless* files are typically not compressed while *lossy* files can be greatly compressed. In printing, it is best to use only the *lossless* file types because of the higher image quality while *lossy* files are well suited for use in web based graphics.

The most common graphic file type is the *TIF* or *TIFF* image (Tagged Image File Format). TIFs are a *lossless* file type designed for cross-platform compatibility and require large amounts of storage space. *TIF* images are *pixel* based, bitmap only files. There is a limit to how big or how small you can scale the file before image quality noticeably degrades. There is a *compression* utility available for use with *TIF* files called LZW, but its use should be avoided because of compatibility issues with some RIPs.

TIF images are bitmaps or a collection of small pixels

Another common file type is an *EPS* (*Encapsulated PostScript*) file which is essentially a self-contained *PostScript* file describing an image including a low-resolution preview. *EPS* files have an advantage over *TIF* files in that they maintain color stability when linked to an application because they are ignored by most *DTP* color management systems. They can also contain a *clipping path* that can be utilized to clip the file when placed in a page layout application. *EPS* files can be either vector or bitmap based. An *EPS* file created in Adobe Photoshop will be bitmap based while an *EPS* file created in Illustrator will be vector based. Vector based *EPS* files are resolution independent and can be scaled up or down with no loss of quality. One drawback to using vector based *EPS* files is that overly complex drawings may be difficult to *RIP*.

File types such as JPG or GIF are *lossy* file types and should be avoided if possible for printed output. Other file types such as PICT, BMP, and WMF files can be used but are known to have incompatibilities with some *RIP* engines.

Keep this in mind

1. Use only lossless file types for printed materials.
2. Understand the advantages and limitations of the file type you are using.
3. Avoid creating overly complex vector based EPS files to reduce RIP time and problems.
4. EPS specific issues:
    - Save them in the BINARY format, not ASCII (reduces file size).
    - If your *EPS* file contains *fonts*, include these *fonts* when you package your files.
    - Avoid nesting one *EPS* file inside another *EPS* file if possible.
    - Reduce the number of points in your vector artwork to a minimum (fewer points does not mean lower resolution, vector art is resolution independent).
    - Don't use the hairline setting for defining outlines in vector files, always specify the outline width yourself, such as .25 points.

> **"File types such as JPG or GIF are lossy file types and should be avoided if possible for printed output. Other file types such as PICT, BMP, and WMF files can be used but are known to have incompatibilities with some RIPs."**

Three basic rules still apply: don't embed your graphics, don't rotate graphics in the page layout application, and don't rename a graphic after it has been linked. All three of these rules will affect your RIP speed or cause graphics to print improperly.

Continuous Tone (CT) image (Photoshop)

CT imported & rotated in Vector Illustration

Final composite imported into Page Layout

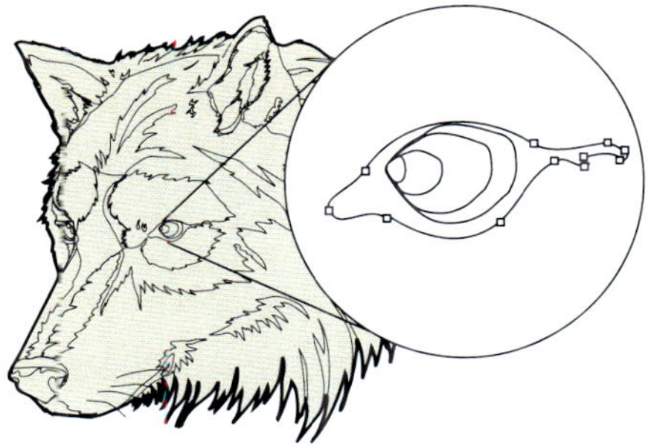

Vector graphics are made up of a series of points and lines defined between those points

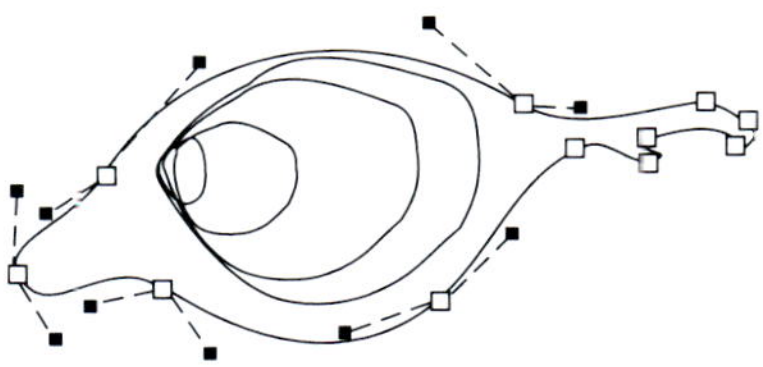

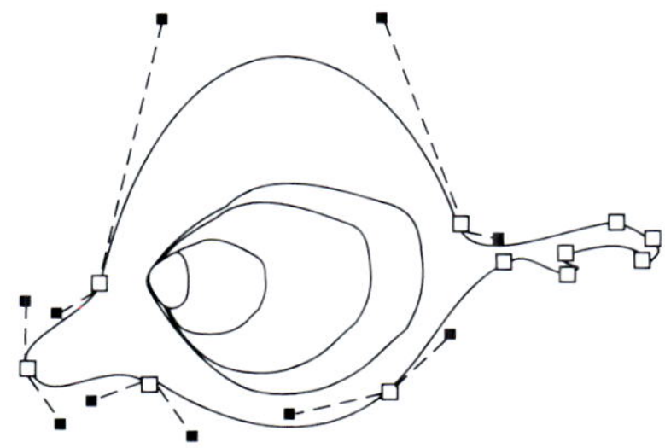

The vector file is changed by moving a point or by redefining the shape of the line between the points

A vector image that is too complex

Proper vector image

Other File Issues

We need to touch on some other general rules regarding graphic files and printing. Following these rules should improve your design workflow, graphic management, and reduce RIP times.

1. When you place graphic images into your DTP software you should link, not embed, the graphic to the application. Embedding a file not only makes graphic management much more difficult but may also increase RIP times.

2. Avoid rotating or resizing graphics in the DTP application. Doing so will increase RIP times. Perform these operations in the graphic editing applications before linking the files. (With today's powerful RIPs, this rule can be somewhat bent, but be aware that you can still overwhelm the RIP).

3. Don't rename your graphics after they are linked to the DTP application. Doing so will break the link causing the low-resolution image to print in its place.

4. After you make any modifications to linked graphics in their native application, you will need to update your links in the DTP application.

Note: *TIFF* images are automatically converted from *RGB* to *CMYK* by some *DTP* applications (i.e. QuarkXPress 4.1). This will cause an unwanted color shift in the output.

Image Capture

The scanning resolution of your graphic images is a complex and confusing issue to most people. Below we explain how to simplify the process.

Original Image Type

There are two basic types of images that you may need to scan, line art and color/grayscale continuous tone originals. These two graphic types are different and need to be treated differently.

A line art image is a binary file and uses only one solid color, usually black. But, line art is also often printed using a specific color or spot color such as in a corporate logo. Line art needs to be scanned at a resolution equal to or greater than the resolution of the printing device.

Continuous tone (*CT*) images (*grayscale* and color images) are images with a continuous tonal range, formatted in a manner that expresses an image. A photograph is a common form of a *CT* image.

Line Art

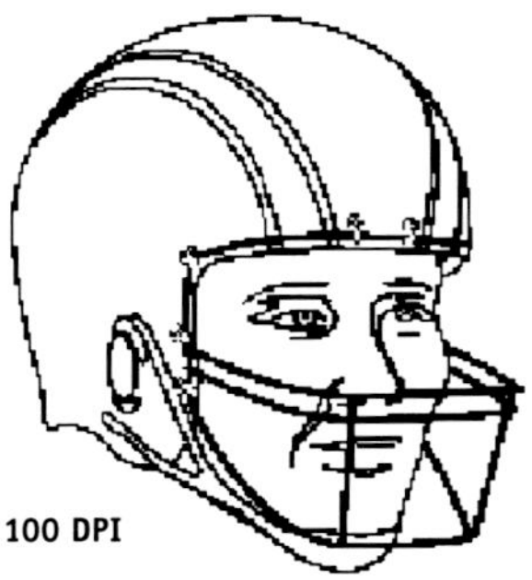

100 DPI

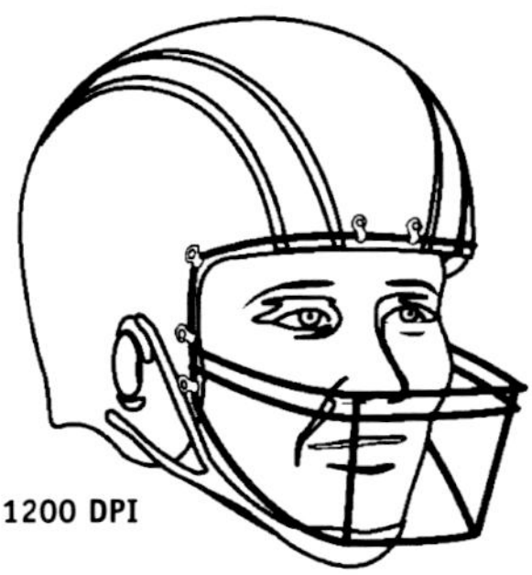

1200 DPI

Scanning Resolution

The resolution at which you scan your images is very important. You do not want to scan at too low a resolution and lose quality, yet neither do you want to scan at too high a resolution—increasing file size and RIP time.

All digital printers create images using a dot per inch (*DPI*) model. A typical laser printer has a 300 to 600 *DPI* output resolution. High-end digital printers may have 600 or 1200 *DPI* output resolutions.

For clarification, depending on where resolution is being measured, it may be represented as *DPI* (*dots per inch*), *SPI* (*samples per inch*), and *PPI* (*pixels per inch*). *Samples per inch* is normally associated with a scanning device, *pixels per inch* with a computer display, and *Dots per Inch* with physical output of some sort. Each of these represents a measurement as units per inch. So, to keep things simple, we will only use *DPI* to represent these in this book.

If you scan a *line art* graphic at less than the output resolution, you risk having the edges of the image appear jagged, or having the "*jaggies*". You may have seen this if you make a non-vector based font too large. So, if you will be printing on a device with a 600 *DPI* output resolution you should scan your *line art* at 600 *DPI* in the black and white mode. For most digital printing equipment, scanning your *line art* at 600 *DPI* should be adequate while 1200 *DPI* should be used for traditional printing processes.

CT originals do not have to be handled the same way. You don't need to scan at such a high resolution to get good image quality. Doing so will make your files extremely large and rarely "better looking"

There is a generally accepted rule for *CT* scanning resolution. Again, this rule was created when computer systems were not very powerful. This rule can be bent slightly to suit your needs, but understand the consequences of doing so.

300 dpi

An image with too low a resolution will not reproduce well

72 dpi

Scan at a resolution twice that of the *LPI* or line screen you are going to use in your printed output. If you are going to use a 150 *LPI* screen, then scan at 300 *DPI*. Always scan at 100% of the final size you need for your output.

DPI of the scanner = *LPI* of the output device x 2

This means that if you will be using a 133 *LPI* screen setting, you should scan the image at 266 *DPI*. Scanning the image at a lower resolution may result in a loss of image quality while scanning at a higher resolution will waste disk storage space and increase *RIP* time.

If you will be scaling the image up or down, making it larger or smaller than the original size, you will need to alter your sampling rate. If you will be reducing the image size by 50% after it is scanned, you can reduce your sampling rate by 50%. If you will be increasing the image size by 30% after it is scanned, you need to increase the sampling rate by 30%. When increasing the sampling rate, we are assuming that the original is of high enough quality to accommodate this.

DPI = *LPI* x 2 x (1 $^{+}/_{-}$ percentage of increase or decrease in size)

133 *LPI*, 150% increase in image size

133 *LPI* x 2 x 1.5 (increase by 50% = 1.5) = 399 *DPI*

Many people simply scan images at 300 *DPI*. This is fine as long as you like the output and it doesn't take too long to *RIP*. If this works for you great, you do not need to worry about scanning formulas.

If your file takes too long to *RIP*, see if your *CT* image sizes are the problem. Will reducing their file size help? Will it affect image quality?

Check with your service provider for their recommendations regarding image scanning. They will know what works best in their environment.

Any image which has been produced using printing equipment, not a picture or negative, is created using a *halftone* screen. This pattern may be too small to see with the naked eye, but it is still there. If you scan such an image, your scanner will pickup the *halftone* screen pattern, possibly creating a *moiré* pattern in the scanned image (an image in which you can see the *halftone* screen more readily). Some scanning devices have *descreening* features to hide this. Always try to scan a *CT* original. If you can't, experiment with your scanner settings to achieve the best results.

It is also possible to descreen previously printed *halftone* images by using the *descreening* feature in a bitmap editing program like Photoshop. You must be careful as this may lead to an image that looks slightly out of focus or soft. The larger the original screen or dot size, the less *descreening* will improve your image. Your service provider with a high-end scanner has much better *descreening* capabilities.

Do you own or have rights to use the images that you are scanning? If not, don't scan them. Every image, whether it is a photograph or a design is owned by the person who created it. If that image has not been placed in the public domain, you cannot reproduce that image without explicit written permission from the owner.

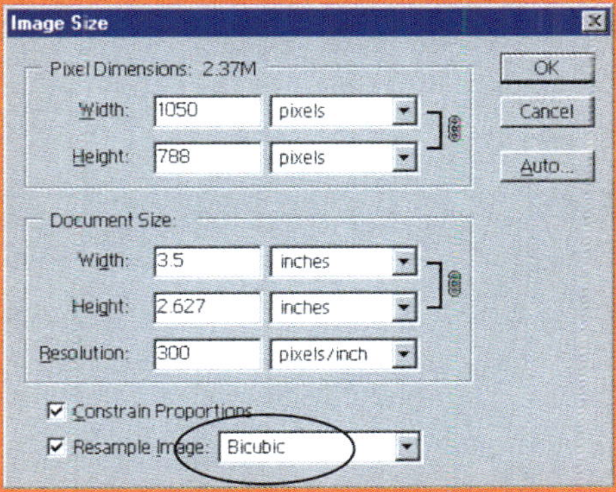

If you must resample, use the Bicubic resampling method, not Bilinear or Nearest Neighbor

As always, when in doubt, consult your service provider.

To increase size 200%
Scanning DPI=LPI x 2 x 2

Resampling Issues

Once an image is scanned, it is stored at a specific resolution and size. Resampling occurs anytime you change the size of an image and cause image data to be discarded or added. So it is possible that an image is resampled when decreasing image size and almost always when increasing image size. You should avoid resampling whenever possible as it causes the re-shuffling of image data and will typically reduce image quality.

Understand that an image is not resampled in Photoshop when you change image dimensions with the "*Resample* Image" box unchecked. As you change the dimensions, the image resolution of the image changes too. So, you are not throwing out data. You must be careful that the *DPI* of the image does not go below your predetermined *DPI* level for output to your chosen device.

Original image — 300dpi @ 2.5″

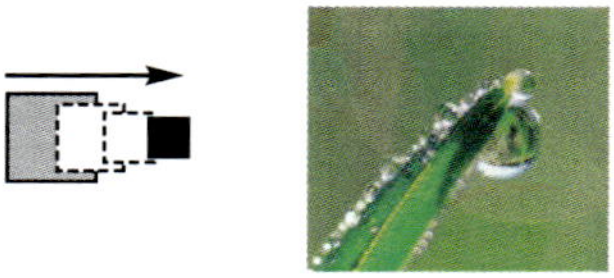

Sampling down to 225dpi @ 1″
No loss of image quality

Resampling back up to 300dpi @ 2.5″
Image quality will degrade

"Avoid any resampling issues by trying to determine the final size of your images before they are scanned. Then scan at the appropriate resolution and scaling factor. You should only then need to make minor changes to your image such as cropping, which does not resample the image."

If you change the image dimensions with the "*Resample* Image" box checked, the image resolution stays constant, the image is resampled, and data is discarded or added.

The addition or subtraction of data is performed in one of three ways: "Nearest Neighbor", "Bilinear", and "Bicubic". Always use the "Bicubic" setting as it is the most advanced method and performs the best job.

Avoid any resampling issues by trying to determine the final size of your images will be before they are scanned. Then scan at the appropriate resolution and scaling factor. You should only then need to make minor changes to your image such as cropping, which does not *resample* the image.

A key consideration when scanning an image is the quality of the original image. You cannot make low quality images better by scanning them at a higher resolution. High quality images can be scanned at higher resolutions. This issue is very important if you intend to increase the size (scale) of the image from that of the original. There are several factors you should consider when looking at the image quality of the original.

- Where did the image come from? The source of the image will generally determine its quality.
- Does the image have good tonal range? Are the shadows dark? Are the highlights bright? The tonal range will also influence how good the image will look when reproduced.
- Is there a color cast? If so, you will have to try and correct this problem in your editing software.
- Is there good lighting in the image? If not, it may prove difficult to reproduce effectively.

All of these will affect the final quality of your output.

Keep this in mind

1. Understand the differences between line art and continuous tone images.
2. Understand the resolutions at which each of these should be scanned.
3. Take scaling into account when scanning an image.
4. Avoid resampling if possible.
5. Take your original image quality into account, you can only reproduce what is there in the first place.

Digital camera

Photographic print or preprinted materials

Photographic negative

3

Design Issues

- Color Crossover
- Trapping
- Solid Fills
- Gradations
- Rich Blacks
- Bleeds and Print Area
- Imposition
- Dot Gain
- Registration
- Total Ink
- Variable Data

Design Issues

DTP applications offer you a myriad of options in creating your work. Many of these options are the same for both digital printing equipment and traditional offset printing, however, you will need to change some aspects of your design to get the best results when submitting to a digital printer.

Color Crossover

A crossover is a graphic that spans two or more pages in a design, usually with a gutter in between. Because the graphic will be printed on multiple pages, it must be carefully positioned in order to line up correctly in the final finished piece.

With a crossover, you need to consider how the piece will be bound in order to determine how to position the graphic. With perfect binding you need to consider the size of the gutter and adjust the inward edges accordingly. This will help avoid the appearance that part of the graphic disappears into the binding. Most service providers will do this for you.

With a saddle stitched document, you need to also consider where in the signature the crossover will be in order to allow for creep. As more pages are added to a saddle stitched signature, you must allow for larger amounts of *creep*.

Be careful with crossover graphics, finishing mis-alignment can cause problems with the job

Keep this in mind

1. Avoid placing small text across two pages because it becomes much more difficult to read as it approaches the gutter. Plus, the horizontal line created by the text will highlight any alignment errors.
2. Try not to use horizontal lines in a crossover as they are difficult to align and will also accentuate any mis-registration in binding.
3. Try not to place crossover art at an angle for the same reason, any mis-alignment during binding will become obvious.
4. Lastly, as always, when in doubt consult your service provider. They've probably dealt with this before and have efficient workflows to deal with your design.

Trapping

Trapping is a term used to describe the manipulation of adjacent color graphics to avoid unwanted visible gaps in the final output.

All printing equipment has a certain registration tolerance. The need for *trapping* is created by variations of equipment tolerances, creating registration inaccuracies when combining the individual color separations (*CMYK*). The mis-registration of one or more inks can result in a gap between adjacent graphics.

You can avoid *trapping* issues by allowing adjacent color elements to share primary colors.

Trapping is a technique of expanding or contracting the boundaries of objects so they slightly overlap. In general, a lighter color expands over a darker color to reduce the chance of gaps being visible in the final output. Expansion of a color is called a spread and constricting it is called a choke.

Trapping can be performed manually, but is rarely done today. In most cases, it is recommended that you allow your service provider to perform the *trapping*. They have sophisticated software and hardware that will most likely perform a more accurate job than you can. There are of course exceptions to this rule.

If you do want to perform your own *trapping*, consult your service provider first.

Too small of type also presents a *trapping* problem. When type is very small (i.e. 8 point or smaller), it becomes very difficult to trap properly. The result may be a noticeable problem on output.

Other techniques included in *trapping* are knockouts and overprints.

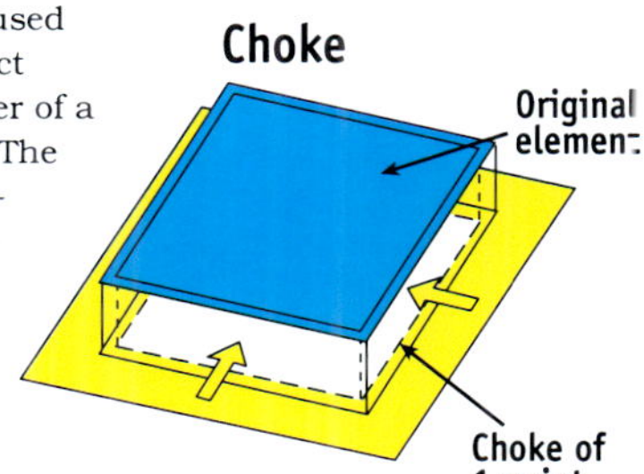

A knockout is used where one object overlaps another of a different color. The knockout eliminates the color beneath the top object. This is done to eliminate the possible color shift that can occur when the two colors are blended.

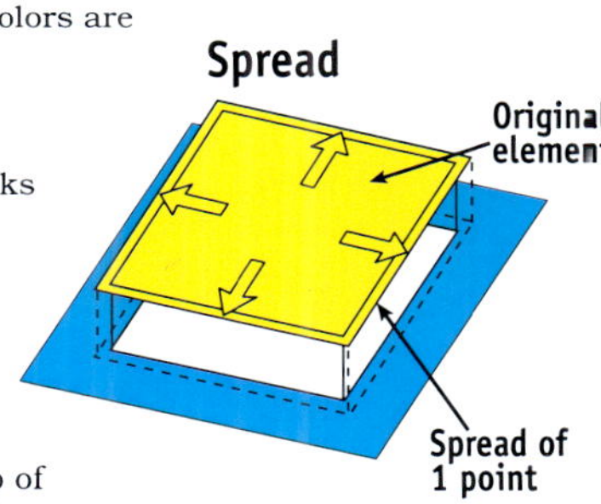

By default, *PostScript* knocks out all objects where they overlap.

Overprinting is printing one item on top of another to create a special effect by the blending of two colors. If you do want to overprint an area, make your service provider aware of what you are trying to achieve. They may see it as a problem and fix or change your design.

Again, leave *trapping* to the service provider, but check with them for good design tips to avoid issues.

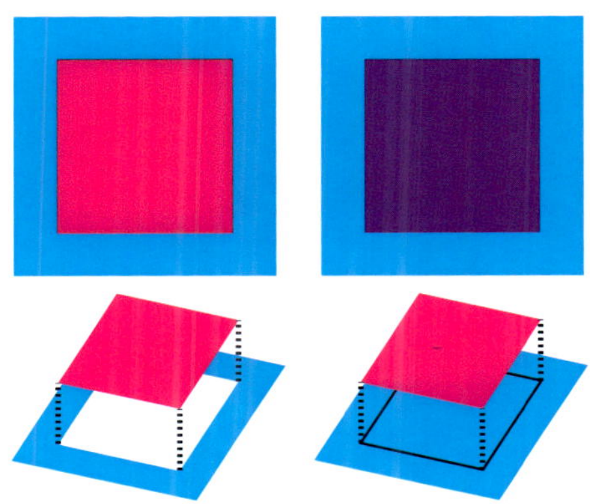

Knockout **Overprint**

Solid Fills

Solid fills or solid areas of color are a common design element that has created problems for digital printing equipment in the past and does so to some extent today.

A digital printing device uses an electrical charge to direct the colorant to the media. Because of variations in the media and the environment, there can be some variability in the charge. This uneven charge has the tendency to create variations in large fill areas.

This is much less of an issue with the latest digital printing equipment and the problem may disappear entirely in the near future.

But, in order to work around this issue today, you have a few choices.

First you can avoid large areas of solid fill in your design altogether. This is an issue with most designers as solid fills are a common design element. One option is to add noise or use a subtle pattern in your fill areas to minimize the visibility of color variations.

The other option is to be careful when choosing your output media. Some digital printers will reproduce fills better on coated stocks while others will do so on uncoated stocks. This is purely the result of differences between equipment. The stock is often the key for each device to effectively reproduce solid fills.

Check with your service provider for their recommendations. They know their equipment and it's capabilities.

Some digital printers may have problems effectively reproducing solid fills on certain media

Gradations

Gradations, blends, vignettes, and gradients are all terms for the same thing, a fill containing a color to color transition or from one density to another.

Banding is an objectionable pattern introduced by the *RIP*. Instead of a smooth transition from one tint to another, you will notice distinct bands in the output.

Most digital printers have an output resolution of about 600 *dpi*. This is lower than most offset printing equipment. Because of the printing resolution, there is a greater possibility of banding in gradations when using a digital printer.

The resolution of digital equipment is improving every year. This will continue to reduce the possibility of banding. Also, the introduction of the *PostScript* Level 3 PDL will help eliminate this issue. Level 3 describes 4096 shades of gray vs. 256 shades of gray available in Level 2.

Gradations created with *spot colors* may appear posterized. To avoid this, create gradations using *CMYK*. Also the application you choose can affect the output.

Keep this in mind

1. Know the resolution of your intended output device.

2. Use a lower *LPI* setting for output. A higher *LPI* setting reduces the shades available for each color.

3. Increase the range of color values used in the gradation to 85% or 90% of the total to increase the number of color shades. A narrow range reduces the number of color shades and causes larger bands in the gradation.

4. Reduce the physical length of the gradation whenever possible. The greater the length of the gradation, the larger the bands.

Consult your service provider for specifics. See if they can suggest a work around.

Process (Rich) Blacks

The use of process blacks is a common way of extending the tonal range of the output device. The idea is simple, add a little of C, M, and/or Y to your solid black areas to improve their appearance. This may also be done to give black either a warm or cool feel.

The use of typical process black mixtures works well with most digital printing devices. Setup your design just as you would for an offset printer.

You may find that traditional rich black mixtures may be too rich for some digital devices. If this is the case, try reducing the CMY color additions to lesser values such as 100K 20C 10M & 10Y or 100K 10C 10M & 10Y. Likewise try reducing the C and M additions for cool and warm rich blacks: cool 100K 15C 0M 0Y, and warm 100K 0C 15M 0Y.

Also, with some digital devices you will achieve your best solid blacks by using 100K with no supplemental color additions. Again, knowing what device will be used to output your work and understanding its characteristics is key.

As always, check with your service provider for specific recommendations about the equipment you intend to use.

0C 0M 0Y 100K

30C 0M 0Y 100K

0C 30M 0Y 100K

30C 30M 30Y 100K

Bleeds and Print Area

You will need to print on oversized substrate if you are creating anything with bleeds. A bleed refers to any printed material where the image or color is printed past the boundaries of the finished page; the media is then trimmed to the final size resulting in an image or color that goes to the very edge of the document. Full coverage documents are created using this method because no printing equipment can effectively print to the very edge of the media on all four sides.

When you use bleeds, you need to take into account the finishing process that will be used for your design. A bleed is typically set to 1/8" beyond the finished page size, allowing enough margin to compensate for inaccuracies in the printing and finishing processes.

You should avoid placing text or graphics at the edge of the page as variations in finishing may give you unsatisfactory results.

Consult your service provider for their recommendations regarding bleeds. Be careful, what may work for one finishing process or printer may not work for others.

Imposition

Imposition is the process of organizing the pages of your design so when the press sheet is folded for finishing, your work will be in the correct page order. Offset printers typically work with very large sheets of paper that can be folded into signatures containing 4, 8, 16, 32, or more individual pages. The maximum size of the press sheet and the size of the finished piece are always factors in the best use of the sheet. Other variables include:

- **Size of finished page**
- **Size of press sheet**
- ***Bleed* or not**
- **Page order**

Most digital printing devices use smaller, cut-sheet paper, so signatures contain fewer pages. Today, signatures from a digital device will typically contain a maximum of 8 pages, but a 4-page signature is the most common.

When a sheet is folded into a signature and stacked within one another, the pages in the middle will be pushed out slightly. This is called *creep. Imposition* software can compensate for *creep* by slightly shifting the images on the appropriate pages inward. When the document is bound and trimmed, all the pages will line up properly. Signatures from digital printers have fewer pages and typically have a smaller incidence of *creep* that must be compensated for.

You can create the imposition yourself or have your service provider create it. Your service provider will have expertise and specialized software capable of compensating for all the variables encountered—while keeping finishing in mind at the same time.

Imposition is one of the greatest influences of a successful or failed job. Don't start a job without considering finishing and *imposition* first. Your service provider will have lots of examples and experiences to share with you.

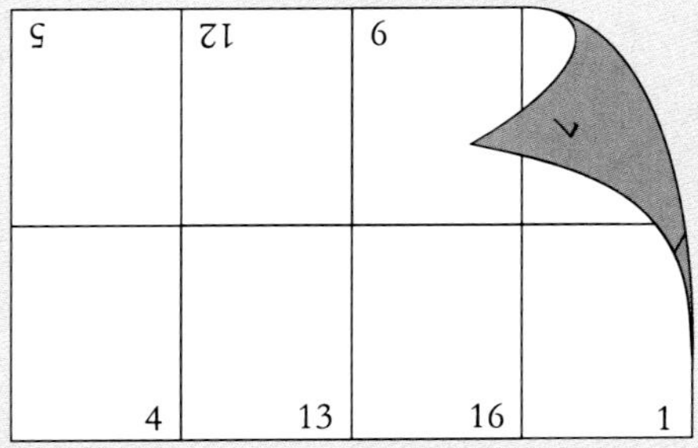

8 up – 16 page signature

4 up – 8 page signature

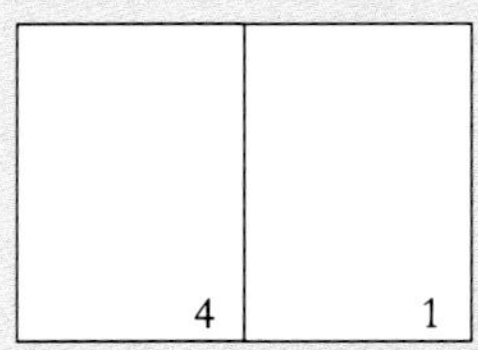

2 up – 4 page signature

Dot Gain

As a colorant is laid down on the media on an offset press, there is a tendency for the ink to spread out as it is absorbed. This is called dot gain. The ink dots that create the image increase in size beyond what was intended. Dot gain can also occur in the plate making process and during image transfer, but most dot gain occurs when ink is applied to the media.

Dot gain can make images and colors appear darker and more saturated than intended. Most *dot gain* occurs in the mid-tones and less so in the shadows and highlights. In shadow areas, the image can plug or fill too much resulting in loss of shadow detail.

A typical offset press will experience about 20% *dot gain*. Most digital printing devices do not use liquid inks, so they typically experience less *dot gain*, about 5% or less. Be aware that digital equipment such as inkjet printers with a liquid colorant base will have *dot gain* comparable to an offset press.

Applications such as Photoshop can be used to compensate for *dot gain* in *continuous tone* artwork, but most *RIPs* will perform this function automatically.

The manufacturers of digital equipment understand that Photoshop is compensating for *dot gain* that does not occur with their equipment. Rather than ask designers to specifically correct for this issue in all their designs, most digital equipment makes the necessary corrections at the *RIP*. So, *conversion* of artwork between offset and digital equipment is unnecessary.

Anyone who prints to a digital device or traditional offset press needs to understand that *dot gain* happens. It may be more or less, but it happens. The media, printing device, and the *RIP* all influence *dot gain*.

Your service provider should test their equipment to determine the affects of *dot gain*. They should then provide you with recommendations for your designs.

50% Screen

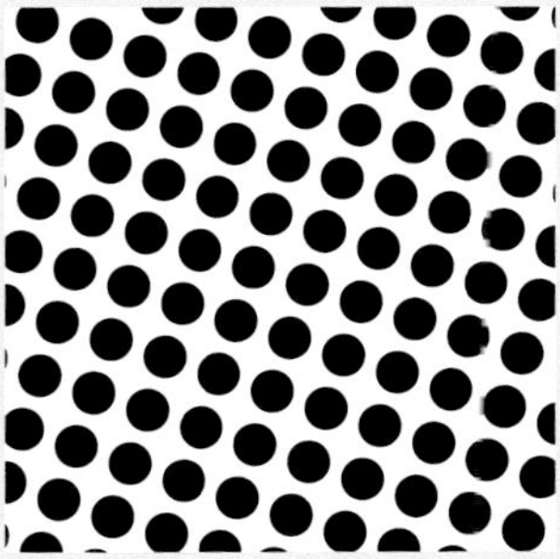

20% Dot Gain

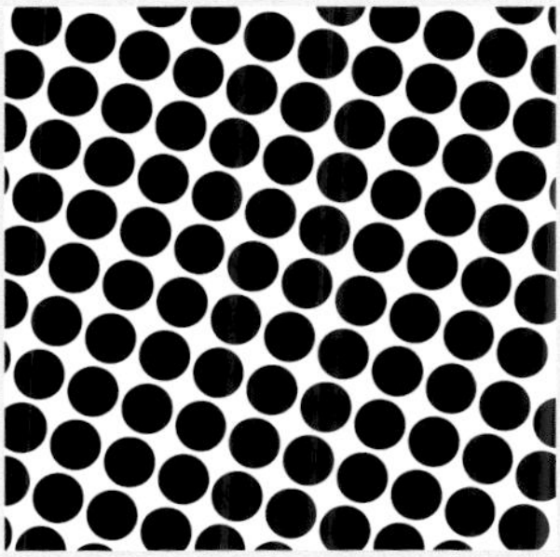

Most digital printing devices experience a minimal amount of dot gain

Registration

There are two types of registration, the registration of ink separations creating an image and the registration or alignment of images between the front and back of the media.

Mis-registration of separations can cause gaps between adjacent colors, degrading the look of the product. *Trapping* is used to compensate for this.

Registration between perfected or duplexed pages can cause objects such as page numbers to not line up, again affecting the quality of the product. Digital printers do not generally offer as tight of registration from front to back as an offset press. However, every digital printer is different.

You may want to take this issue into account with your design. Check with your service provider for specifics.

"Imposition is one of the greatest influences of a successful or failed job. Don't start a job without considering finishing and imposition first."

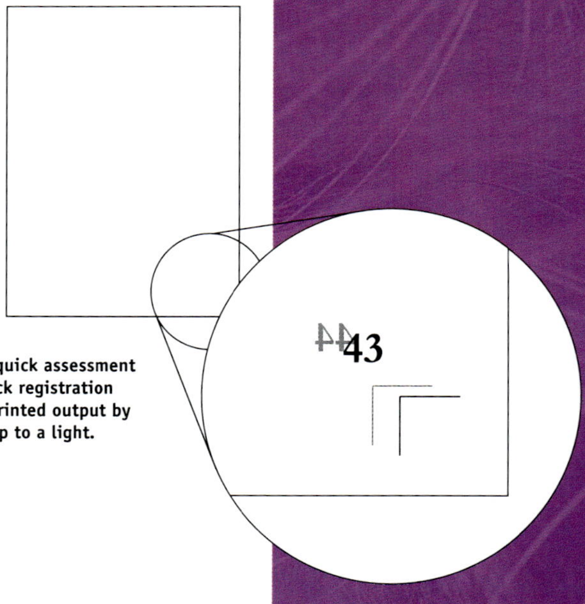

You can make a quick assessment of front to back registration errors on your printed output by holding it up to a light.

Total Ink

Total ink refers to the combined amount of ink or colorant used in a printing process. This primarily concerns continuous tone images. With process colors there is a maximum possible total ink limit of 400%: 100%C, 100%M, 100%Y, and 100%K. However, most systems won't print using total 400% ink coverage.

All printing systems have a maximum total ink limit at which images can reliably be created. This amount is also partially determined by the media used.

Newspapers, because of the porous media, have a total ink amount of about 240%. Most digital printers operate between 240% and 280%, but some go as high as 325%. *SWOP*, the industry standard in the offset printing world, uses a total ink limit of 300%.

The total ink limit can be manipulated in a variety of places along the production path.

Check with your service provider for their recommendations regarding total ink settings to obtain the best output quality.

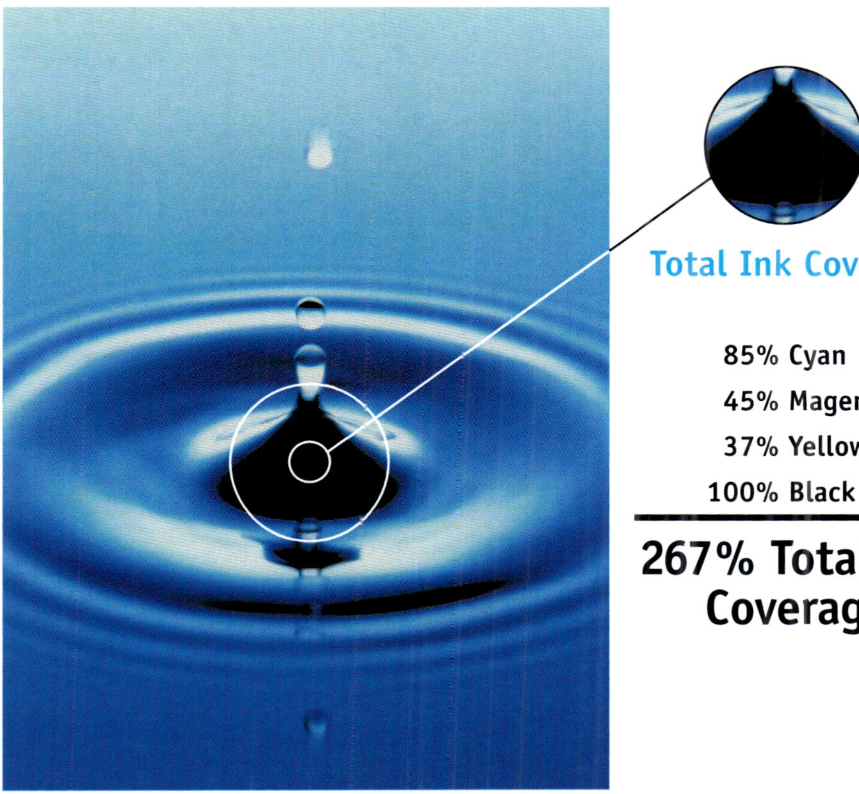

Variable Data

Variable data printing (VDP) is one of the hottest topics in the printing industry today because it offers the ability to change the data being printed on each page. Digital printing is the only printing technology that truly offers this capability.

VDP is important because it offers companies the ability to individualize promotional documents, providing each potential client with information tailored specifically to them. It gives marketers the ability to address consumers on a 1 to 1 basis. VDP is commonly used for creating marketing literature but is also used for creating transactional documents such as financial statements.

VDP comes from two capabilities: the ability of the *RIP* to create images at a speed equal to or faster than the printer and the ability of a digital printer to print unique data on each page.

VDP requires the creation of a base form and a client information database. The base form is typically created in a page layout application and the client data is generally gathered from a mainframe computer database. The database information may be manipulated and converted into a data form that is more compatible with variable data applications.

VDP comes in three basic forms: stand alone off the shelf applications, applications typically bundled with a *RIP* and a custom programmed application.

Each type offers specific capabilities and attributes. Some may be very easy to use but lack certain capabilities. Others may be powerful, but are complicated and require a trained programmer to operate.

All vendors of digital printing equipment offer the capability of VDP, however, not all service providers have moved into this market.

Again, check with your service provider regarding what they have to offer, chances are they can accommodate your needs.

Keep this in mind

Several design issues need to be addressed differently when dealing with a digital printing device:

1. Solid fills, will your traditional methods be effective?
2. Gradations may need to be be altered.
3. Rich blacks may be different.
4. *Imposition*, smaller sheet size, smaller signature size.
5. Registration may not be as accurate as with offset printing.
6. If your design is later re-purposed to an offset press, only minor changes should need to be made.
7. Bottom line, know the device you intend to use and create your design accordingly.

4

Printing Issues

- Choosing the Right Printing Equipment
- Printer Capabilities
- Media Quality
- Printer Speed and Job Cost
- Output Media Size and Related Finishing Options

Printing Issues

Just as there are different types of printing equipment to choose from, there are different levels of output quality from which you can choose. Each quality level has its own advantages and disadvantages as well as differing costs.

The Xerox DocuColor 6060 Digital Press

Choosing the Right Printing Equipment

The main variables you must deal with are the output quality you desire, the length of your print run, and the money you are willing to spend for your job. An old printing industry adage states: "Your choices are Quality, Speed, and Price. You can choose any two you want!" If you want high quality and speed, the cost will be more, or if you want speed and a cheap price, the quality will be lower. With digital printing, you may be able to have all three.

Printer Capabilities

Print quality is typically driven by two factors, printing process and media. LPI represents the lines per inch the press manufacturer is able to reproduce with their equipment.

Most commercial digital printing systems use *Lines Per Inch* (*LPI*) to represent the line screen that can be generated, and typically use line screens between 133 and 200 *LPI*. Don't confuse *DPI* with *LPI*. *DPI* (*Dots per Inch*) represents the smallest dot that a digital press can effectively create. Most digital printers and presses operate between 600 and 2400 *DPI*. *LPI* represents the line screen that the press is able to generate. There are many *Dots per Inch* representing each halftone cell (dot cluster) in a line per inch screen.

The *LPI* rating for a printer is always less than *DPI* rating for that printer.

175 *LPI* allows the reproduction of fine detail and good over-all quality. This is

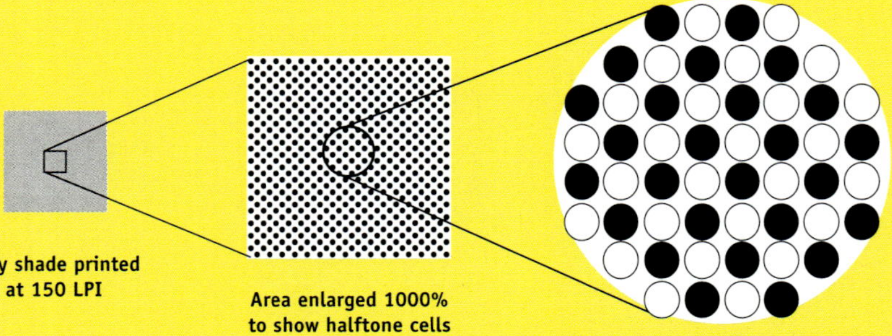

Gray shade printed at 150 LPI

Area enlarged 1000% to show halftone cells

Area enlarged 400% to show dots creating the halftone cell (DPI)

generally adequate for most print jobs. The majority of the general public will not be able to see the halftone cells creating the image at 175 *LPI*. Be careful about getting too obsessed regarding image quality. Yes, image quality is important, but if your client is satisfied with the image quality and is willing to purchase the job, it is good enough!

Media Quality

The media you choose will also affect output quality. There are several thousand varieties of media to choose from, each is different and each has specific characteristics and costs. Higher quality media costs more, possibly much more. Again, the output quality you desire will drive you to use specific types of paper. If you only need to convey a message, but are not too concerned with the appearance of the job, a lower quality media may be acceptable. However, if you need your final output to be of higher quality, you will need to choose a high quality stock.

Every printing media has a limitation to the image quality it can hold. Newspaper is a very porous material and will not hold a small dot. As the ink is absorbed and spreads on the paper, dot gain can be very excessive. This is why newspapers are printed between 80 and 100 LPI.

Higher quality printed images, as in glossy magazines, are printed on higher quality or smoother, non-porous paper that can hold a smaller dot. Often times magazines are printed with screens between 150 and 300 LPI. The harder and smoother surface of the paper is less porous and does not allow the ink to absorb and spread on the sheet. Consequently there is less dot gain and the result, with the higher line screen, is a higher quality image.

The media used for printing also has a significant affect on color reproduction. Paper reflects un-absorbed light back to the viewer. The more reflective the paper surface, such as a coated paper, the wider the potential range of colors that can be reproduced. Using a less reflective paper will result in a narrower range of potential colors.

Some digital presses utilize roll as opposed to sheet fed media

Not all white paper is pure white. Some papers have a blue or a yellow cast. The color cast of the paper will affect the colors perceived in two ways: First, colors are often applied as percentages (shades) in a design. This allows light to penetrate the color and be reflected off the paper picking up the color cast. Second, the paper cast of any areas where no color is applied will affect the perception of adjacent colored areas (adjacency affect).

Consult with your service provider regarding their equipment capabilities and compatible stocks.

Media Issues

Not only should you understand the quality of the media to be used, you must also understand that most digital presses put much more stress on media than a traditional offset press.

First, most press manufacturers create a recommended media list for their product. This is a list of all media types that have been tested and certified to run acceptably in the printer. Typically this list will contain information such as paper manufacturer, model number and name, size, weight, color, etc. It may be possible to run stocks not on the list acceptably on a printer, but the manufacturer will not certify the output results.

Many digital presses use heat and pressure to fuse the image to the media. These forces can convert excess moisture in the media into steam, creating image quality problems with the output.

Most digital printers use some form of electrostatic charge to create an image. A key issue to consistently controlling this charge is to control the temperature and humidity in the press room. Too low of humidity can cause potential feeding and image transfer problems. High temperature and high humidity can easily create problems.

You need to keep in mind stock acclimation. Media spends much of its life in uncontrolled environments such as warehouses and trucks. Imagine what kind of issues would arise if you took paper from a truck in sub-zero temperatures and immediately ran it through the press. The results would be unsatisfactory. Media must be allowed to acclimate to the conditions of the press room before being printed. A pallet of paper can take over a week to fully acclimate.

Many digital printers utilize high temperatures to fuse the image to the page. Some use temperatures as high as 400 degrees Fahrenheit. If the media contains too much moisture when it passes through the fuser, the moisture can be instantly converted into steam and ruin the image. Also, the high heat can actually cause the media to shrink slightly when fused. If the job is perfected, the stock is subjected to these stresses twice.

Digital printers also place a lot of stress on the media. The typical paper path of a digital printer is full of tight turns, starts and stops. This is tough on the media and can cause problems with some stocks. To help deal with this issue, most digital presses feed stock with the grain running perpendicular to the paper path. This may cause issues when finishing the job. Consult your service provider about how certain media might behave in a given process.

Again, this is an instance of how digital printers place high stress on the media. Consult your service provider for their recommendations.

Printer Speed and Job Cost

Printer speed and job cost are often inter-related. Every printing device has a speed at which it is rated to operate and an associated operating cost. Job cost is most often determined by the print quality required, job turn around time, and print run length. These in turn relate to printer capabilities and printer speed.

After considering print quality, the next questions you need to answer are: "How quickly do I need this job completed and what am I willing to pay?" These questions will drive you to specific printing equipment and specific costs.

As far as printer speed, you must use equipment that is fast enough to meet your turnaround time requirements. A slow printer will probably cause your print job to be late.

Different printing equipment has differing operating costs at given quantities. Producing short run jobs on an offset press may prove uneconomical, while running a large job on a digital press may also prove cost prohibitive. If the cost of the job is important (When is it not important?) choose the right equipment for the job.

Typically, a digital printer is best suited for shorter run jobs. Short run jobs can be defined as any job requiring between 1 and 2000 sets. This number is relative, ask a dozen people their definition of a short run job and you are likely to get a dozen different answers. Variable data jobs can fall under the short run category (job length of 1) or much longer.

Every model digital press has its own capabilities. Consult your service provider regarding the output options they offer and what best suits your budget.

Output Media Size and Related Finishing Options

Output media size is an important consideration in determining the final cost of your job. With offset printing you can print on virtually any media of varying sizes. This is not the case for digital printing equipment.

Not all media types are compatible with digital equipment and media sizes are typically limited to 12x18 inches and less today. These media limitations may affect your choice to use a digital printer.

As we discussed earlier, bleeds will cause you to utilize media larger than your final piece. However, depending on the size of your work and the capabilities of the equipment to be used, image *imposition* may be able to save you money.

Imposition may allow you to reduce the cost of the job

"Your choices are Quality, Speed, and Price. You can choose any two you want! In the near future, digital printers may allow you to have all three options with little or no sacrifice."

If your project can be imposed in a 2up or 4up arrangement, you can cut your costs dramatically, because your service provider can use larger media sizes and thus run fewer pieces through the printer. If you choose to go this route, you should probably insist on having a digital press proof to assure quality. If the job will require additional folding with *imposition*, test this as well.

The best thing is to discuss this option in detail with your service provider before you begin to design your piece. This way you may be able to make small, subtle changes to your design and possibly save some money.

Keep this in mind

1. Choose the right equipment for your job. The wrong equipment may increase your costs or create other issues.

2. Quality first, "How good does it need to look?" or "What are you willing to pay?"

3. Remember, the media is a big part of the final quality.

4. Turnaround time. How quickly do you need the job completed? How much does the affect the cost?

5. Job cost. How much do you have to spend on the job? Can you meet this budget?

6. If you decide to output the job with a lesser quality, will this be noticed by the end users and do they really care?

The answer to these questions will point you in the direction of the equipment best suited to your needs.

5

Printing Color

- Device Gamuts
- Color Models
- Process, Hybrid and Spot
- Printing Elements
- Color Management Systems
- Consistency Verification, Calibration, Characterization, and Conversion
- ICC Profiles
- CMS and DTP Applications

Printing Color

Creating high quality color printed images is a very complex subject that cannot possibly be discussed in detail by this book. Because of this, we will only cover some basic issues regarding the color printing process.

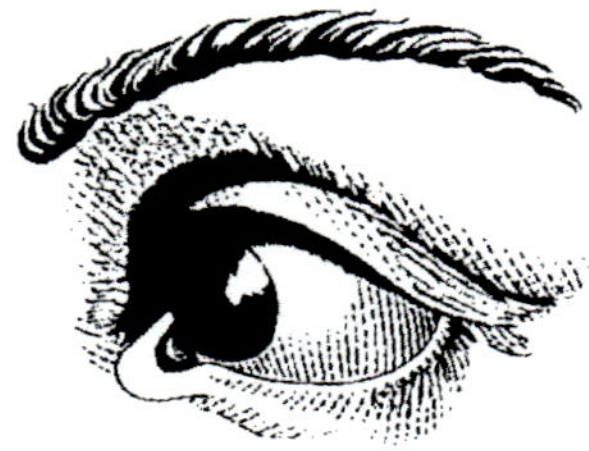

The human eye has the largest gamut of anything in the color workflow

Device Gamuts

The range of colors that can be represented, captured or reproduced is called a color gamut. Every device used to produce printed materials has its own unique color gamut.

We can see more colors than a photo can represent. In other words, the gamut of the human eye is much larger than the gamut of the color photographic process.

The color photographic gamut is larger than the gamut captured by an *RGB* digital scanner.

Most digital scanner gamuts are larger than the gamut of a computer monitor.

The monitor gamut is larger than the gamut produced by *CMYK* digital color printing equipment.

The digital color printer gamut is generally larger than the gamut produced by a *CMYK* offset printing press.

All of these are generic representations, but they are generally accepted as accurate. There will always be cases where portions of a gamut will overlap a superior technology, but when taken as a whole, the assumptions above are realistic.

The strengths and weaknesses of your intended printing device gamut should be taken into account with your designs. (i.e. Does the device produce great purples or reds? Use those colors in your design and avoid the weak colors.) Speak with your service provider regarding the gamut range of their output devices. They may be able to suggest specific colors that work better than others.

Color Models

The color we see on printed material is created by what is called the *subtractive* color model. When light strikes an object, it is either reflected or absorbed.

Subtractive colors absorb certain parts of the light spectrum and reflects others. When we see a red apple, it is not because the apple is emitting red light, it is because light waves other than red are being absorbed by the surface of the apple while the red portion of the light spectrum is being reflected to our eyes. Printed materials absorb and reflect light waves in the same way creating the colors we see. The colors created by a digital printer are specific to the factors that define the process (colorant, substrate, printing method), making the result device dependent.

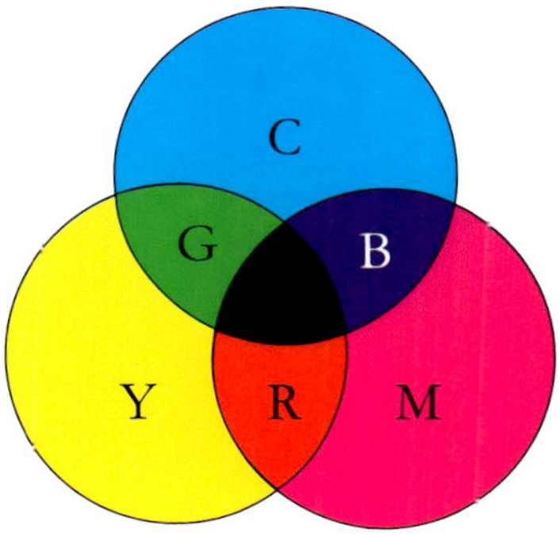

Subtractive Primaries

Images created on a computer screen are created in the opposite way. A monitor uses red, green, and blue colored phosphors to create color images the screen. Energy causes the phosphors to glow. Varying the amount of energy acting on the phosphors allows the monitor to create shades of different colors. This is called the additive color model since combining the three primary colors in varying amounts creates different colors.

A computer monitor is capable of displaying a larger color gamut when compared with printing equipment.

Many of the colors displayed on your *RGB* monitor will not be the same when printed. Typically, colors produced on a monitor must be compressed into the gamut of the printing device, possibly shifting the colors and altering the look of the design.

Your monitor simply provides you an on screen estimation of your printed work. Unless you are using a color managed monitor that has been modified to look like your printing process, don't expect the colors you see on the monitor to match your printed output. What you see is NOT necessarily what you get, but

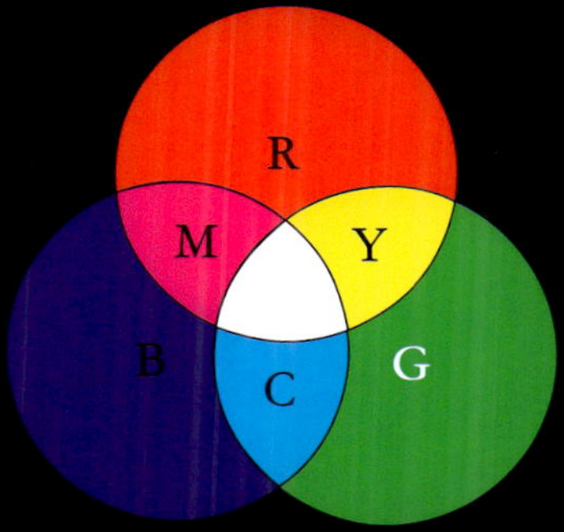

Additive Primaries

it may be close enough for your needs. You may need your service provider to create a proof copy of your file in order to get a better idea of the final output.

Process, Hybrid and Spot

Printing color can be accomplished by a variety of methods. The most common color printing method uses what are called process colors. Process colors are created by mixing a combination of four colors: Cyan, Magenta, Yellow, and Black (CMYK). With these four colors, you can create a range of many colors. Not all CMYKs are the same. Cyan from

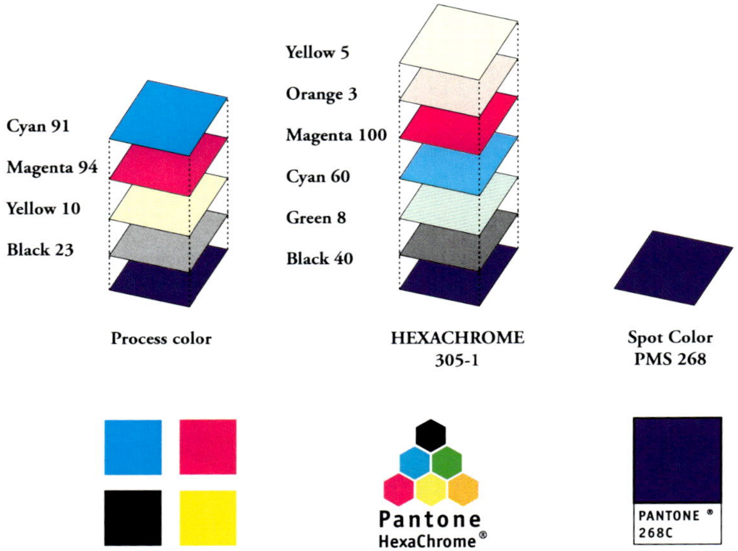

A similar color produced three different ways, CMYK, HexaChrome, and a Spot color

one vendor to another can be slightly different. Don't forget the influence of the media on the final colors, changing the media can change the perceived color gamut.

Because some colors are not easily achieved by the use of process colors, some manufactures have developed systems that utilize *CMYK* plus additional colors. These hybrid systems can use a total of five, six or even seven individual colors to produce an image. The advantage is a larger printable gamut. The downside is increased complexity of the equipment and the software driving the system. As with most things, the more complex a process, the more difficult it is to control and the greater the chance of system failure.

The last method uses what are called *spot colors*. *Spot colors* are made to achieve a specific resulting color. These colors are specified by one of the spot color systems, such as the Pantone Matching System (PMS), and are designed to achieve a close match between the specified color and the final output. The use of *spot colors* is very important when printing designs that require reproduction of specific colors as in corporate logos. Using a premixed or spot color can reduce the chances of the color shifting during the job. Most digital printers do not truly support spot color printing today.

Spot colors are typically simulated on digital printers when a true spot color cannot be utilized. A *CMYK* recipe is substituted to simulate the spot color.

Be aware that some digital printing devices can print black & white, color, or both. The cost for printing B&W and color is different. If you prepare a print job for B&W output, but you include any color graphics, the job will automatically print in color and you will be charged more for the print job. The solution to this problem is to either convert all your graphics to *grayscale* images (black & white) or be very specific when defining your print job and emphasize that it is to be converted to B&W output.

Let your service provider know if your job is B&W, color, or both.

Printing Elements

When you create your designs with most prepress applications, you will be defining your designs using CMYK, RGB, Spot colors, or Grayscale elements. These elements may be text, graphics, continuous tone images, gradations, screens, fills or others. Regardless of the element, it will be defined by one or more of these colorspaces.

CMYK is the traditional method of defining non-spot colors in the printing industry. It is a known quantity that can produce excellent results in most situations. Designers have historically based their color designs on the CMYK model.

Today, most designers understand the characteristics of CMYK and how to manipulate images to achieve the desired result. We use what we know works.

Technology and the ways in which documents are created is changing this. Today, most RIPs can also accommodate elements in the RGB colorspace (this was not the case 10 years ago). Also, many documents are being repurposed to use on the Internet. Internet information is displayed on computer screens in RGB. The use of some RGB elements (scanned images) in your designs may prevent you from having to create and color adjust two completely different image sets, both CMYK and RGB.

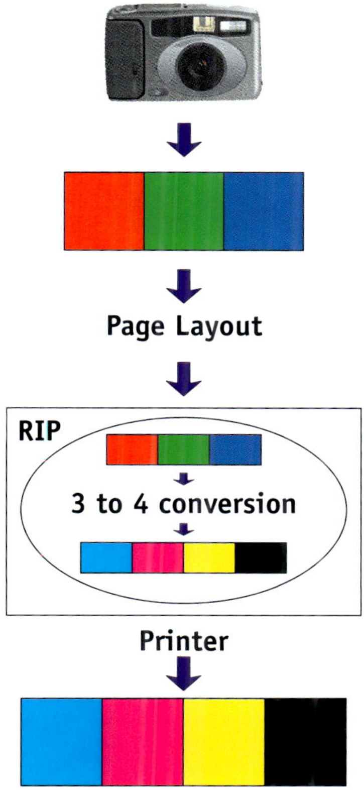

A digital printer can efficiently accept RGB input directly to the RIP

There are some distinct advantages to incorporating RGB elements into your designs. First, all scanners and digital cameras capture images in RGB because of the technology. Some of these devices will convert the image to CMYK for you, but it is still captured in RGB. Second, image editing applications such as Photoshop offer more features and options when working with RGB images, giving you more control. Lastly, the RGB gamut is larger than traditional CMYK. Depending on your output device, you may be able to achieve a wider range of colors and a more realistic reproduction of an image by using an RGB image.

Remember, some of the newer digital printing devices offer gamuts larger than traditional CMYK color combinations such as SWOP.

For many designers it is more difficult to edit images in *RGB* than in the *CMYK* colorspace. It may take some time, training and experimentation to become proficient at editing images for print in *RGB*. We are not suggesting you switch to an *RGB* workflow. But, be prepared to work with people and systems that may be using an *RGB* workflow.

Today, you can design in a variety of hybrid color systems (more than four colorants) but very few digital printing systems currently support this option. Even if the press does support a hybrid system, it may be proprietary. If you intend on using a hybrid color system in your design, discuss this option with your service provider in detail to avoid confusion and problems.

Other elements that require a specific color match may require the use of a spot color. Some digital devices can accommodate this through the use of a true spot color. Most digital devices mimic *spot colors* by referencing a spot color dictionary (*color rendering dictionary*) to match the color as closely as possible using *CMYK* combinations. Some digital printers are even certified by spot color manufacturers to acceptably emulate certain *spot colors*.

The last element at your disposal is black. Black is used in most designs for text and some graphics. It is not expected the use of black in printing will ever disappear.

There is a place for all four elements in today's workflows, *CMYK*, *RGB*, Spot, and Grayscale. In your designs, use the element that offers the most flexibility, economy, and potential in order to maximize your work.

Printing Adjacent Colors

You need to be aware of issues dealing with linework elements of differing colorspaces. This is only an issue if you intend for two items to appear the same color in the final output.

Pantone Purple C
CMYK recipe differences

	Adobe Photoshop 7.0	QuarkXPress 5.01
C	45	38
M	82	88
Y	0	0
K	0	0

In a perfect world you could use equivalent measures of CMYK, spot, and RGB in adjacent elements. But, as you know, printing is not a perfect world!

You need to keep in mind that even though a spot color is converted to CMYK when printed, chances are a CMYK element and an equivalent spot element will not appear the same when printed (i.e. a spot fill adjacent to an equivalent CMYK gradation).

This is because the CMYK element is passed through the RIP as is. On the other hand, a spot color call-out is passed through the spot CRD (color rendering dictionary) and converted to CMYK. Chances are the spot conversion to CMYK is slightly different than the CMYK equivalent specified in your layout application.

The CMYK representation of the spot color is different in the spot CRD because these colors are tweaked by the RIP manufacturer to obtain the best representation of the spot color for that device.

In addition, remember that any CSA or ICC profile attached to a graphic may force the element through a color conversion in the RIP changing the final color.

Keep this in mind

1. Understand the gamut capabilities of the device you intend to use.
2. Understand the printing capabilities of the device.
3. Understand process, hybrid, and spot colors.
4. Understand the advantage and disadvantage of utilizing color elements in different colorspaces.
5. Understand the dynamics of adjacent elements of differing colorspaces.

Color Management Systems

The complexity of preparing color files for printing and the variability of color printing processes make it almost impossible to produce exactly the color you want. Don't forget, the human eye can see millions of colors but most color printing systems can render only several thousand individual colors. It is impos-

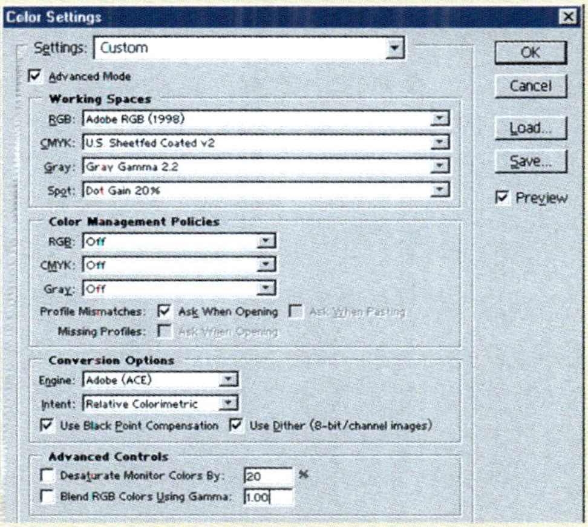

Color settings in Photoshop 6

sible to have absolute control over the color printing process.

To gain some control over this process, you can utilize a color management system (CMS). The purpose of a color management system is to make your output match the original design as closely as possible.

Because color management is a complex process, it is not well understood or utilized properly by many organizations. Large service providers may have experienced personnel and use color management in a "closed loop" system where they have complete control of images and output, start to finish. This takes a substantial investment of personnel and money.

In an "open loop" system where print jobs come from outside sources, true color management becomes more difficult or almost impossible. This is because content creators have a variety of CMS tools at their disposal. Perhaps they may or may not know that decisions they make can affect the color management or the process. The result

is like a group of carpenters building a house with sacks over their heads, no one knows exactly what the other person is doing or has done.
In the most successful workflows, content creators and service providers work together to manage the entire process.

There are different types of color management systems: proprietary systems and color management systems that utilize color profiles (ICC profiles or tags) for each piece of equipment used in the creation of a job. This equipment includes scanners, digital cameras, monitors, and most output devices. These profiles, one for each device, are embedded into a digital file to provide information about the color characteristics of the equipment used in creating, editing, or outputting the file.

The profiles allow for accurate conversion of color gamuts from the scanner to the monitor, and finally to the output device. Any color management system utilizing ICC profiles involves four basic steps: consistency verification, calibration, characterization, and conversion.

Consistency Verification, Calibration, Characterization, and Conversion

Consistency verification refers mainly to the printer and is the process of assuring it is operating in a consistent manner within manufacturer specifications. This is sometimes also called normalizing, linearizing or standardizing the printer. If the printer is not operating in a consistent, stable manner, the colors of a file printed today will be different than the same file printed at some point in the future.

Calibration is the process of measuring and adjusting the performance of a device. Any device in the workflow may be calibrated if this capability was designed into it. Calibration brings the performance of the equipment into an expected range and is generally performed with the use of a densitometer or a spectrophotometer. A densitometer measures the density of the colorant on the specific substrate while a spectrophotometer measures the actual color produced. Calibration for a printer should be performed on the specific substrate that will be used to print the job because the substrate affects the colorant density and the substrate will have a color that can affect the perceived color of the final piece.

Just as a musical instrument requires tuning before its use, so does a digital device. Digital printers need to be regularly calibrated in order to provide consistent results.

Characterization is the process of defining the color gamut of a specific device. Each device, scanner, monitor, printer, or digital camera has its own specific color gamut. These color gamuts will be different for two identical pieces of equipment because of subtle differences in hardware, software, and environmental influences.

Devices are characterized by creating a color profile (ICC profile) for each device. A special color target is output on the digital device and then measured with a spectrophotometer. An ICC profile is the result of this process.

Conversion is the last step. Conversion is the process of converting the color gamut of one device to the color gamut of another device (i.e. from the scanner to the monitor, or from the monitor to the printer). Data from the source device is moved to an independent colorspace such as CIE L*a*b. Then it is converted to the gamut of the destination device. This conversion is controlled by the characterization (ICC profile) of each device.

A color managed workflow is a complex undertaking. Its success or failure is not however totally determined by technology. The key component to the success of implementing and maintaining a color managed workflow truly depends on the commitment of company management to the process. Without management support, any color managed workflow is destined for failure.

ICC Profiles

If you choose to implement an ICC profile workflow, you must use software during the design and printing process that supports them. Most newer DTP applications support working with ICC profiles, older versions may not. It is important that you identify the specific software settings required to properly utilize the color profiles in your workflow. Failure to do so will result in unpredictable (not color managed) output.

In an open loop system, most of the problems occur when an inappropriate profile is applied to an image and inserted into the workflow. As the image moves through the system, colors are converted to different device gamuts, causing unwanted color shifts to occur and resulting in the wrong color in the final output.

Utilizing ICC profiles in a color managed workflow requires education, experimentation, and special equipment and software to work properly. If you choose to utilize a CMS in your job, make sure you involve your service provider and communicate your methods and the desired out come.

CMS and the DTP Application

Many people perform color management within the DTP application with an output profile for the printer being applied as the final step. Many RIPs also offer the capability to apply a

An IT8 color target can be used to create an ICC profile

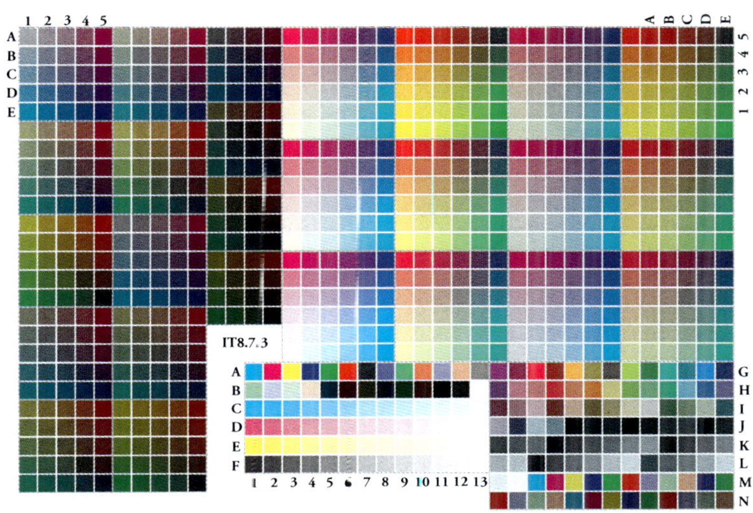

profile to a print job. It is important that the output profile not be applied in both locations (apps and RIP) or you may get unexpected results. If you choose to perform your color management at the DTP application you should disable the CMS settings at the RIP.

Check with your service provider for their recommendations and carefully read the documentation for your applications.

Many DTP applications also include generic color profiles in their color management system. Because you do not know the conditions under which these profiles were created, you will not know the results of their use until you run test prints.

The other option is to disable the CMS at the application level and enable it at the RIP. With this arrangement, you will probably want to keep your workflow as simple and consistent as possible.

Most RIPs include generic output profiles and rendering intents to manipulate your files and obtain specific results. These output profiles are not specific to your machine and will not provide specific results when utilized (this is an uncontrolled method of managing colors). You may also be able to change the CMYK color curves and alter the colors of your work.

No matter what output options you choose or CMS options are applied in your DTP application, your service provider can override these at the RIP. Operator choices at the RIP take priority over virtually all document settings! Make sure you understand the typical methodology of the service provider and clarify your needs.

Regardless of what form of color management system is utilized within your organization, two things are very important:

- document a step-by-step process of your preferred workflow

- instruct everyone to follow that workflow

These two simple steps will greatly improve your quality and your customer's satisfaction.

Keep this in mind

1. If you do not truly understand color management, don't use it.

2. The four Cs:
   Consistency verification
   Calibration
   Characterization
   Conversion

3. A bad ICC profile can ruin a good job.

4. Know where your CMS is being applied in your workflow and how to use it properly.

6

Preflight

Manual Preflight

Preflight Applications

Web Preflight

Preflight

In this book we have discussed many ways to correctly prepare your files and have identified some things you should avoid. The main purpose is to create your files in a way that will produce "good" *PostScript* and give you fewer problems when you output.

Preflighting is essentially a structured method of checking files to ensure they are well prepared before being sent to the printer.

Manual Preflighting

One method of preflighting a design is to do so manually. With this procedure, you open up the design files and review the parts used to create the file. You are looking for:

- No locally stylized fonts
- No missing fonts and graphics
- No graphics that have been rotated or resized in the page layout app
- No graphics with too high or low of resolution
- No mixing of font types, etc.

Many problems can be identified and fixed using a manual preflight method. The result of this effort should be a better file that prints successfully.

There are two downsides to manually preflighting designs: you have to know how to efficiently operate the DTP applications and it is a time consuming process.

First, you have to have the expertise with the applications used to create the design in order to be able to identify problems. People with this skill level are not cheap. You need an expert level designer with a good working knowledge of at least half a dozen graphics applications. Wouldn't it be more profitable to have them performing other tasks?

Also, manual preflighting takes time. In the printing business, who has enough time? Do you want to invest half an hour of labor only to find that your customer's file is unprintable and must be reworked? Time is money, isn't it?

If you manually preflight your designs before you ship them to the service provider—great! That is exactly what you should do. Better yet, if the files are created properly the first time around, then the time and effort to preflight will be less.

If you are performing the service provider functions and are preflighting someone else's files, manual preflight is probably not cost effective.

Check with your service provider for recommendations. Usually they can share some effective suggestions regarding file design and preflight.

Manual preflighting requires extensive application knowledge

Preflight Applications

An option to manually preflighting a design is to use a preflight application. Several manufacturers offer these applications with a variety of capabilities and costs. Markzware and Extensis are examples of companies that offer preflight applications.

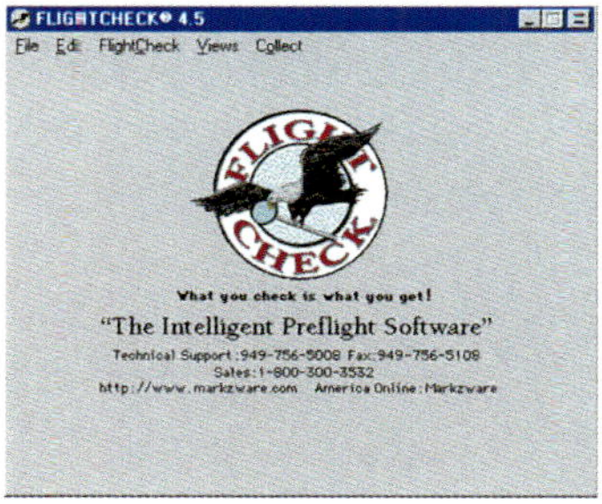

FlightCheck by Markzware is a popular preflighting application

Specialized preflighting software can examine a design and all related files, then create a report identifying potential problems. Most of these applications let the user set priorities of items to be examined, allowing for customization to your specific needs.

Most large service providers have and use preflight applications in their daily operations. In general, it is cheaper to run all designs through a preflight application instead of wasting valuable RIP time on poorly prepared designs. Some service providers even make the use of a preflight program a requirement for print job submission.

Check with your service provider regarding their recommendations and capabilities.

Web Based Preflight

A relatively new development to preflight applications is web based preflighting.

As more and more service providers are offering web based file submission services, they are also able to incorporate preflighting.

The typical web based preflight setup works as follows: A user uploads a design for submission to the service provider. While they are waiting for a reply such as a job ticket number, a preflight application is examining their design. If the design passes the predefined preflight parameters, a job ticket number is returned to the user. If the design does not pass preflight, the preflight report is returned to the user detailing problems that must be addressed before re-submission.

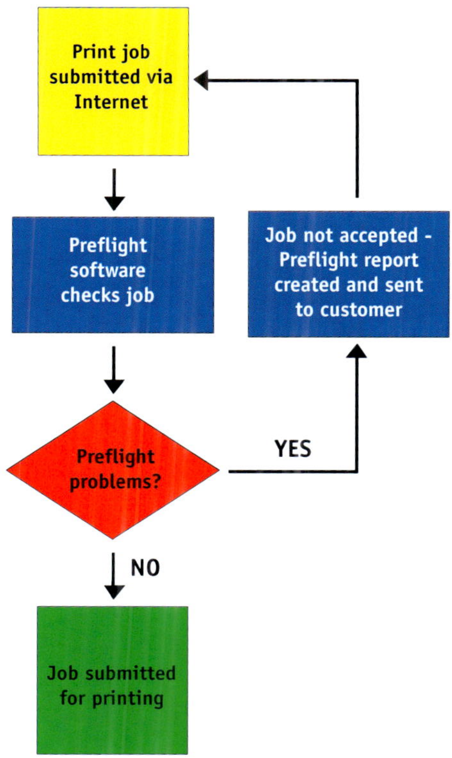

Web based preflight flowchart

This system allows the service provider to ensure that any file coming from their web submission system has been preflighted. The service provider should then have better success printing jobs and should be more profitable.

Your service provider may or may not offer this service.

A preflight application is a fantastic use of technology that can make us more efficient and provide us with more time for other tasks.

If you work for a design firm or a service provider, your company should probably make use of some sort of preflighting software. The initial cost of the application is quickly recovered when fewer hours are spent manually looking for problems in designs and more jobs can be run successfully.

For more information and an in-depth look at preflighting, buy the book, *Preflight: Avoiding Costly Printout Problems Through Proper File Preparation*, by Peter I. Muir.

7

Submission

Native Application Files

PDF Files

How to Create a PDF

Using Adobe Acrobat Distiller

Print Ready Files

PPDs and Settings

Submission Options

There are several formats you can use to submit your designs to a service provider. We will be discussing types of files, not methods for transporting them.

The three commonly used submission options are native application files, PDF files, and print ready files. Any of these options may be valid, but the service provider usually requests the option they prefer.

Native Application Files

The first option is to use an application file created by your DTP application. Another name for this is a source file. There are advantages and disadvantages to using this file type.

The primary advantage is the ability to make changes to the design required for proper output. This assumes the service provider has the same application and version. You may be charged for this service depending on the type and complexity of the problem.

A primary disadvantage is the need to send the layout file, the fonts and all graphic files. If you leave any items out, your service provider will not be able to properly print your job.

QuarkXPress is a popular page layout application

Submitting application files is fairly straightforward and is one of the most common methods used today. Follow the submission requirements established by your service provider.

PDF Files

The next option for sending your work to your service provider is a PDF or portable document format file. The use of PDFs is growing in popularity. The PDF is a document type developed by Adobe Systems and is a derivative of PostScript.

The popularity of PDFs is due to a number of reasons:

- *PDFs* offer a smaller file size.
- They are platform independent allowing them to be used with multiple computer systems.
- If created correctly, a *PDF* will contain all graphics and *fonts* used in a design, simplifying file submission.

But, the use of *PDFs* does have a downside. The biggest problem service providers have with *PDFs* is a limited ability to fix problems. Because a *PDF* is basically *PostScript* code in a nice wrapper, there is a limited opportunity to edit them. There are specialized applications such as Enfocus' Pitstop that allow you to look at how the *PDF* is created and identify colorspaces, *fonts*, etc. This application also allows you to make some changes to the document such as editing text, colors, even replace objects in the design. But in general, you do not have the same control over the design as with the source file. If there is a problem with a *PDF*, the service provider may require it to be corrected by the designer and re-submitted.

How to Create a PDF File

There are a few methods used to create a PDF.

The first method is to create the PDF directly from the DTP application. Some applications support this, some do not. Also, not all applications with this capability do a good job of creating the PDF. You have to test this feature to determine its effectiveness.

Some applications such as Illustrator, Photoshop, and InDesign allow you to save your design directly to the PDF format. This is typically done with the "Save As" command.

Other applications can create a PDF with the "Print" dialog. With this method, you will usually go to your print dialog box, make the selections that you would for normal printing, but select "PDF Writer" for output as opposed to printing. Now when you print the document, the application will ask you to name the PDF and to specify a storage location. Be cautious when using this option due to limited functionality and the quality of the resulting PDF.

The second method of making a PDF is more complicated, but offers the most flexibility and is the most reliable. This method involves creating a raw PostScript file and using Adobe Acrobat Distiller to create the PDF. With this option you can control every aspect of how the PDF is created.

This method is also the most reliable because you are utilizing the strengths of your applications (PostScript code created directly from your application and PDFs created using an application specifically designed for that purpose).

Be aware that using the wrong Distiller settings or print driver and PPD can ruin the resulting PDF.

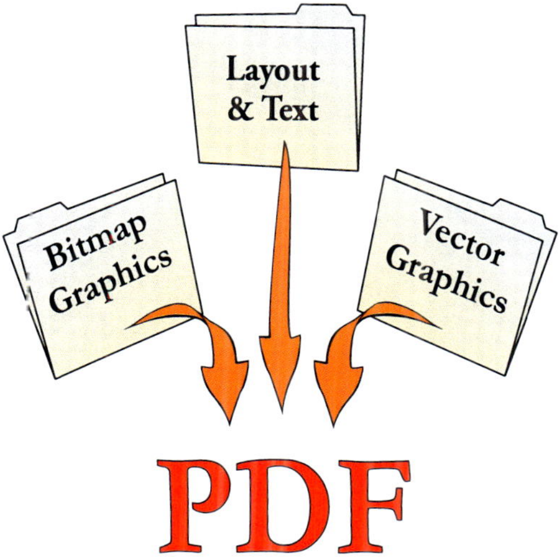

A well prepared PDF combines all the graphics and fonts used in the design into one file

You may also find that this is the only reliable method of creating printable files (work around) from office applications such as PowerPoint.

Utilizing Adobe Acrobat Distiller

As stated earlier, Adobe Acrobat Distiller is an application designed specifically to create PDFs. Even though it is specialized, it offers a relatively complex selection of options. It is important that you understand these options and use them appropriately. The best place to start is to talk with your service provider.

You have to first create a PostScript print ready file. See the next section for details regarding this.

Upon launching Distiller, you are offered a selection of output options. Examples are 'screen optimized", "Print optimized", and "Press Optimized". Version 5.0.x also offers "e-book" as an option. Screen optimized is used to create low resolution PDFs intended to be viewed on a monitor; they do not have a high enough resolution to print well.

Print optimized is used to create PDFs with enough resolution for most printing situations. This option typically down

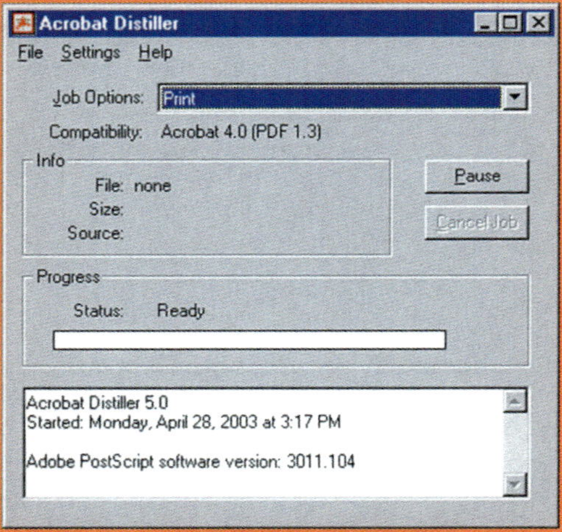

Adobe Distiller Screen

samples graphics to 300 DPI (you can set the Distiller options for other resolutions). Your selection should be based on the print resolution of the output device.

Press optimized uses resolution settings that would be typical if outputting to an offset press. These settings may cause long RIP times on some digital output devices.

Distiller also has a number of color options available. These options can significantly change the colors of the document if used incorrectly. See the "help" document supplied with Distiller to help explain these settings.

For advice on what specific settings to use with Distiller, first check with your service provider. They should know what works well for their equipment.

For additional information, go to the Adobe web site, www.adobe.com. Search for a document called, "How to create Adobe *PDF* Files for Print and Press". This document will give you very specific information regarding settings in Distiller.

Learn all you can about *PDFs*, you will probably be using them more frequently in the future.

Print Ready Files

The last option for job submission is to create a PostScript, "print ready" file. You should only use this method after you have checked with your service provider, they may or may not be willing to work with these.

With this option, you create a PostScript file using the specific printer description file for the output device. The file created is printer dependent and will contain all of the graphic images and fonts you have used. You will not have to include these files separately.

The reasons you may want to use this option are:

- You are going to use an application such as Adobe Acrobat Distiller to convert the *print ready file* into a *PDF*

- You will be sending the *print ready file* through some additional prepress (*PostScript*) process

- You will be submitting the *print ready file* directly for output

Creating a Print Ready File

It is very important that you use the correct printer description file (PPD) for the destination printer when creating your print ready file.

For most applications you will utilize a PPD in conjunction with a printer driver such as a Laser Writer driver. The PPD is used to define all of the output options for the printer.

Once you have installed the appropriate PPD, open your application and your job file. When you are ready, choose "File/Print". At this point you will be presented with a menu box that allows you to select your printer and printer options. Select the printer you will be using for output.

The computer system you are using will determine the options you are presented with To make things even more confusing, these options vary slightly from application to application. To keep it simple, just remember you are simply printing your file, it is just being converted to a computer file as opposed to being sent to a printer.

So, set your file up exactly as you would for printing. For the output device, choose "print to file" in your dialog box. If your application does not offer a "print to file" option, you need to setup your printer driver with the output option of print to file as opposed to printing to a network destination. Refer to your help menu if required.

When setting up your print ready file, the options you select define the information contained in the file. You get what you send! If you choose the wrong options, you won't get what you want. This is probably the biggest problem you will encounter with the use of print ready files, you do not know what your file will look like until it is output (unless you will be creating a PDF).

Be sure to select all the proper options for printing. Be thorough, don't leave anything out.

These options will include:

- Paper size
- Paper orientation
- Paper type
- Printing resolution
- Font options
- *PostScript* options
- Bleeds
- Registration
- Positioning
- Etc... (there are many choices as there are output options for the printing device!)

Most of these options will have fairly obvious choices. If you are not sure about some options, check with your service provider.

Two printing options you should pay particular attention to are fonts and PostScript options. For fonts, choose the option of "Always send fonts to printer". This will embed all the fonts into your print ready file reducing font problems at the RIP. For PostScript options, choose the highest PostScript level available (level 2 or 3), assuming your service provider supports these options. These higher PostScript levels will take advantage of newer PostScript capabilities when the file is created. Most other PostScript options should be left at their default settings unless you are instructed to do otherwise by your service provider.

You may also have a printing resolution option available (this may not be available because the printer driver is specific to the printing equipment and is automatically set to the proper resolution). Check with your service provider about this option. In general, you will want to choose the highest possible resolution available for the equipment being used for your print job.

Once you have selected all of the appropriate printing options, you can choose "print" to create the file. Once you choose "print", you will be asked to provide a name and location to store your *print ready file*.

You can now send this to your service provider by whatever means, disk, CD, or Internet, or use this file to create a *PDF*.

Print ready files are an output option available to you. They may or may not be appropriate for your situation. Check with your service provider for their recommendation.

Keep this in mind

1. Check with your service provider for what output option they recommend and support, native application file, PDF, or print ready file.

2. If you submit an application file, package your design properly and include all fonts and graphics.

3. If you submit a PDF, print a color proof, check it over carefully, and supply this with your file.

4. If using Distiller, be careful about what options you choose.

5. If you supply a print ready file, make sure and use the correct PPD and output settings.

6. Make sure and download all fonts into your print ready file to reduce problems.

8

5 Digital Printing Tips

5 Reasons Why Output Fails

5 Digital Printing Quick Tips

This section offers 5 tips for optimizing your designs for digital printing equipment. Digital printers work differently than traditional offset presses. There are some issues you should be aware of when designing your work. For more information, refer to the relevant chapters and the glossary.

1. Design for Digital Printing

First, if you know your design will be output on a digital printer you should optimize your design for that device. Like a press, every digital printer will have certain capabilities and limitations. Speak with your service provider to find out about the system they will use to output your design. Ask them about any specific recommendations or specifications to keep in mind. Take these into account when designing your work to ensure the output you receive is what you expect.

2. Consider Finishing Options

Many printed items require some type of finishing before completion such as cutting, folding, or binding. Since most digital printing devices create the image in a different way than ink based printing, the finishing options change slightly.

Images from digital printers may not fold well because the surface bonded toner will have a tendency to crack and flake off. Design your work so graphics do not cross fold areas or use light coverage in these areas instead. If your design does cross a fold, scoring the media before folding may help reduce possible cracking. Coating or laminating the cover before folding can also help prevent this problem, but it will also increase the total cost of the job. Check with your service provider as to which stocks and specific coatings or laminates work the best for your application.

If you intend to bind the document being printed, pay attention to the grain of the paper. The binding of your document should be parallel to the grain of the paper, not perpendicular to it. The grain of paper is the direction in which the paper fibers are oriented. With 8.5" x 11" cut sheet paper (not covers) the grain will normally run parallel with the longest edge (called "grain long"), while with covers and larger stocks, the grain will normally run parallel with the short edge ("grain short"). This will allow the paper to lay flat for a better binding. With a cover, having the grain direction parallel to the binding will allow the cover to lay open while binding against the grain will cause the cover to snap shut when opened.

Consider the end use of your document before you create it. Allow this to drive your finishing choices, and thus some of your design parameters.

3. Pick the Right Paper

There is a wide variety of media types available to offset printing. Not all of these are based on wood pulp. Generally, not all substrates suitable for offset printing are compatible with digital printing technologies. Poly based stocks (transparencies, etc.) may be a particular problem.

A smooth, premium white paper is generally the best choice. This is because the colorant used by most digital printers is bonded to the surface of the paper as opposed to ink, which soaks into the paper. A smoother paper will provide a smoother surface to which the colorant can bind, providing a higher quality image. Avoid recycled paper stocks, as they will generally have a heavy texture and may have loose fibers that can contaminate the digital press. Also, some digital printers have problems with coated stocks.

Stock weight is also an issue. Some digital printers will perform better on lighter as opposed to heavier stocks while other digital printers can easily handle 100-lb. cover stock. Check with your service provider for specifics.

Lastly, there can be problems with the moisture content of the paper and the amount of paper dust present. Moisture in the paper can create problems for most digital printers. Make sure that your service provider stores their paper in a climate controlled area (constant temperature and humidity) for at least 24 hours before use. All paper has a certain percentage of paper dust present, but some paper will have much more dust than others. Using paper specifically designed for digital printing equipment should give you the best results. Again, your service provider can provide you with information on these issues.

If you want to produce your job on a stock your service provider has no experience with; it would be wise to run a pre-production test to ensure compatibility. Never test new stocks with your production run.

4. Solids, Blends, and Colors

Digital printers typically use a colorant that has specific electrostatic properties to create an image. Many digital technologies utilize these characteristics to move the colorant to the substrate.

For this reason digital printers may not print large solid areas of color/tints or blends as well as other types of printing equipment (this will become less of an issue with continued improvements to digital printers). Some people compensate for this issue by adding noise in the flat areas using Photoshop or other software. This tactic may correct the problem but it may also make your solids look splotchy. You may need to experiment a little in order to determine which options are best for you. Check with your service provider for recommendations.

Digital printers do not create images quite the same way as a traditional press. You may find that it is difficult to create smooth transitions throughout gradations, blends, or vignettes when using some substrates. You can add noise or apply a gaussian blur to these with your bitmap editing software to make the variations in these blends less noticeable. Also, watch gradations from very dark to very light colors, as these will cause the most problems (there is more specific information on gradations earlier in the Design Issues chapter).

Although most digital printers can produce a larger process color gamut (larger range of colors) than most offset presses, many today cannot print true spot colors because they typically utilize only four colorants. However, the larger CMYK color gamut of digital printers allows them to reproduce more spot colors than ever before. With the most current digital printing devices, the recommended workflow is to use spot color call-outs in your design (i.e. Pantone Matching System colors). The RIP should then recognize these call-outs and reference the specific spot color from a color rendering dictionary. This will provide the most accurate color match on the final output. Also, avoid changing the names of any spot colors.

If you want to print large black solids, it may be helpful to use a variation of the "rich black" *CMYK* settings common to offset printing. Different digital printers have different tolerances for rich blacks. Some digital printers will produce a richer black by adding some CMY to the mix while others may produce the best black using only 100K. Try 30C 15M 15Y 100K or even 10C 0M 0Y 100K for some devices. Your service provider should be able to aid you in selecting the correct mix.

5. Registration

Designers familiar with offset printing may be accustomed to tight front to back registration. Digital printers will not usually (today—2003) be able to maintain similar tolerances. A typical digital printer can maintain about a 1 or 2 millimeter registration tolerance. Run a test document to determine if this will be a problem with your design. You can then decide if you need to change your design or consider a different printing system.

Take these tips to heart and design your work to suit the capabilities of the device you will be using. You will be more satisfied with your final product.

5 Reasons Output Fails

There are many reasons your file may or may not print correctly. Here is a list of the top 5 reasons why you may not get what you expect.

1. Missing Fonts

Font problems will undoubtedly cause you and your service provider more headaches than any other prepress issue. You will benefit by paying particular attention to your fonts.

If possible, use only one font type in your work and preferably use Type 1 fonts. These are a de facto standard in the printing industry and their characteristics are well known to most service providers.

After Type 1 fonts, your next choice will most likely be TrueType Fonts, especially if you are working on a PC based computer. TrueType fonts are acceptable by most, but not all, service providers. Check with yours to find out.

TrueType fonts used with an office application may also reflow if the printing device defined during layout is different from the final printing device. A work around for this is to determine what printer will be used to output your files and establish this as your default printer in your PC from the start of your design. The fonts should then not reflow when sent to your service provider. Reflow can happen in other instances also, watch out for it. Submitting a PDF file is another method of preventing text reflow.

Additional font types include the newer Open Type fonts. Be aware that not all service providers will be able to support Open Type fonts at the time of this writing.

Lastly, when you package your files for submission to the service provider, create a folder called "Fonts" and place a copy of all the fonts used in your document in that folder. Also, if using Type 1 fonts, be sure and get both the screen and printer fonts used and include any fonts embedded in graphic files. This is the typical/accepted methodology, however, your font manufacturer may not allow you to do this legally. Read your font licensing agreement to be sure and check with your service provider for their recommendations.

2. Graphics Problems

The graphic files used in your artwork are commonly next in line as the most troublesome items. The main issues are missing graphics, graphics with lost links, only low resolution graphics, graphic files with too much resolution, or the wrong file type.
Missing graphics are a problem because people forget to include all of their graphics when they submit their work. Again, create a folder called "Graphics" and be sure to include all of your graphic files in that folder. Layout applications may also lose the link to a specific graphic if it is moved to a different location; be sure and check graphic links before sending.

Many times when people are working with low resolution (for position only or FPO) images, they forget to include all of the high resolution artwork when submitting their job. In this case the job will print but the graphics will be incorrect because only the low res images were printed. Be sure to include your high resolution artwork.

Too much resolution can also be a problem. There is a ballpark resolution for scanning your continuous tone images. The generally accepted rule is two times the LPI of the final output. This is about 300 dpi for images that will not be scaled up or down. Why 300 dpi? Scanning images at a lower resolution may result in too low a resolution in the finished piece resulting in poor image quality. Too high a resolution creates very large files that must be ripped resulting in possible processing problems. Also, every RIP/printer combination has a resolution at which an image can be reproduced. If you send an image with too high a resolution, the extra data is discarded anyway.

Remember this, scan your images at a resolution at which there will be no visual degradation of quality and at a resolution that can be easily handled by the RIP (there is more on this earlier in the book). If in doubt, consult your service provider, wait...consult them anyway. They really don't mind answering a question that will help them with their work.

3. Embedding EPS Files

Embedding an EPS file within an EPS file can also create problems. When this is done, an extremely complex image may be created, which creates much more work for the RIP and can cause the file to process improperly. An example of this might be if you were creating a design in which you placed an EPS clipart of a flower bouquet in another complex EPS. The problem is that the bouquet design contained ten thousand vector points. You have increased the complexity of your design and it will take longer to RIP. Today's faster RIPs are better able to process such files, but you can't be sure until you run the file.

Also, it is possible to embed a vector image that contains a font call. If you do not include this font in your Fonts folder, there is a good chance a font substitution will occur and your file will not look correct when output.

Bottom line, avoid embedding EPS files into EPS files when possible.

4. Complex Vector Files

Vector files are nothing more than a series of points and mathematics defining the image. It is possible to create a vector file containing so many points it will not RIP successfully.

Solution: Simplify your graphics when possible, fewer points, fewer gradients and patterns, no extra information etc. (fewer points does not mean lower resolution, vector art is resolution independent).

5. Image Colorspace

Digital printers can deal with several types of colorspace data: RGB, Spot colors, CMYK and grayscale. This capability offers some distinct workflow advantages such as a larger colorspaces and more accurate reproduction of certain colors. But, the advantage can also be a burden to those who fail to understand that each colorspace can be translated differently and yield unexpected results.

Some spot or RGB data lies outside the gamut of the printer in question. In order to print this information, colors are converted to the closest colors within the gamut. This may produce a visible change in the image, producing unwanted results.

To complicate matters further, some or all of this data may have color profiles attached, altering the result of the color conversion. In addition, the operator can choose to honor or discard these profiles at the RIP.

Depending on your workflow requirements, you can choose to take advantage of colorspaces other than CMYK, deal with potential color shifts, embed profiles or not, and to honor or discard these profiles at the RIP (as well as a few additional RIP options). Yes, this is complicated, but, it can offer you distinct workflow advantages.

In the end everything gets converted to CMYK whether it's a spot color or RGB color from a scanner or digital camera. Most RIPs make decisions on how color will be converted from spot to CMYK or from RGB to CMYK, or even CMYK to CMYK. Taking the time to understand how your RIP handles color conversions, what operators should do and how content creators should prepare files will go a long way to helping you set color expectations and increase your productivity.

Summary

In this book we discussed a wide variety of prepress subjects for preparing designs to be output on digital printers. But, we only scratched the surface. Remember, this is meant as an introduction to prepress methods only. It would take volumes to adequately discuss most of the chapter topics in depth. And then, advances in technology would make the contents out-dated in a matter of years or months.

Advancement in printing technology is what makes this business so interesting. It is constantly changing around you, opening up new opportunities and closing others. It keeps you on your toes.

If you want to learn more on any particular subject, do some research, search the web, buy a book, or attend a seminar. There is an almost limitless amount of information is available regarding the printing industry.

The graphic communication industry is the third largest in the world behind food and clothing. Graphic communications is how we share ideas and knowledge. Through it, we have learned most of what each of us knows.

Now that you have all of this information, what can you do with it?

If you are the designer, you can use it in your own file preparation. You will create better files and get better resulting output. If you are the primary or intermediate service provider, you can use this information to help educate your customers on how they can achieve the best quality with the least effort. This will help them create better files and you will have fewer printing issues as a result.

The main idea is to help your customers improve their workflow and work habits so that they can achieve the results they desire. You as the service provider will benefit in your efforts because your customers will be more satisfied with your service and probably send you more business.

Internet Links/Book Titles

Below are some Internet web links where you can find additional information.

Software

Adobe—www.adobe.com
www.adobe.com/print/prodzone/
www.adobe.com/support/techguides/main.html
QuarkXPress—www.quark.com
Colorspace Calculators—www.brucelindbloom.com

Hardware

Apple Computer—www.apple.com
CREO—www.Creo.com

Education

Rochester Institute of Technology—www.rit.edu
GAIN-GATF—www.gatf.org
International Color Consortium—www.color.org
Color Gear—www.chromix.com/colorgear
Apple Computer—www.apple.com
Ollé—www.olle.com
www.about.com (desktop publishing)

Design

AIGA—www.aiga.org
Creative Mac—www.creativemac.com

Index

Book Titles

Below are some book titles on related subjects.

Preflight, Avoiding Costly Printout Problems Through Proper File Preparation, by Peter I. Muir.

The Very Last Designers Guide to Digital, On-Demand, and Variable-Data Color Printing, by David Clark and Frank J. Romano.

Print Publishing Guide, The Essential Resource for Print Publishing, by Adobe Press

Registered Trademarks and Trademarks

Adobe Photoshop
Adobe Illustrator
Adobe InDesign
Adobe Pagemaker
Adobe Framemaker
Adobe Distiller
Corel Draw
Corel WordPerfect
Corel PhotoPaint
Enfocus Pitstop
Extensis Preflight Pro
Macromedia Freehand
Marksware Flightcheck
Microsoft Word
QuarkXPress

Glossary

Absolute Colorimetric - The intent is to maintain color accuracy at the expense of preserving relationships between colors. Used for company logos and where a specific color must be reproduced as closely as possible. It leaves colors that fall inside the destination gamut unchanged, but out of gamut colors are clipped.

Aliasing - The stair stepped or pixelated appearance of low resolution computer graphic images. This can occur when a graphic image is scaled up (increased in size) beyond what the image resolution can support, allowing the individual blocks of data to become visible.

Anti Aliasing - Digitally adding successively lighter pixels to the edges of diagonal lines to hide digital stair stepping.

Additive Color - This is the method of producing color used by all color computer monitors, televisions, and projections systems. The three additive color primaries, red, green, blue, (RGB) are used in combination (added together) to create the colors we see.

Bit - A digit of binary information represented by a 0 or 1, and is the basic building block of all computer system data.

Bit Depth - The amount of data required to represent the tone depth of a color. Typical bit depths are 1 bit for line art, 8 bits for grayscale images, and 24 bits for RGB color images, and 32 bits for CMYK color images.

Bitmap - The image created by representing computer image data as individual dots on an X/Y plane.

Bleed - When an image is printed past the boundaries of its final size (the image bleeds off the edge of the paper). The media is then trimmed to the final size resulting in an image that goes to the very edge of the document. A full bleed extends on all four edges of the sheet.

Clipping - The color shift caused by the inability of one colorspace to reproduce all the colors of another colorspace. When using absolute or relative colorimetric rendering intents, values from the source gamut outside of the destination gamut are forced (clipped) into the destination gamut. Colors within the gamut of both colorspaces are left alone. As a result, two colors that were originally different may now share the same values. This produces visual color shifts.

Clipping Path - A vector path attached to a graphic or continuous tone image. The path hides (or clips) areas that are not to print.

Calibration - The process of measuring and adjusting the performance of a device. Calibration brings the performance of the equipment into an expected range and is generally performed with the use of a densitometer.

Characterization - The process of defining the color gamut of a specific device. Each device, scanner, monitor, printer, or digital camera has its own specific color gamut. Devices are characterized by creating a color profile (ICC profile) for that specific device utilizing a spectrophotometer and special software.

CMYK - Cyan, Magenta, Yellow, and Black. The subtractive primary colors used in printing color images. Also known as process colors.

Color Management System (CMS) - Software systems used to ensure color consistency among different input and output devices so printed material will closely match originals.

Conversion - The process of adapting the colors produced by one device to the colorspace of another device and takes place anytime information is passed between devices (i.e. from the scanner to the monitor, or from the monitor to the printer). Colorspace conversions are performed in device independent color-spaces such as CIELAB or CIEXYZ.

Color Profile - A file containing the color characteristics of a computer device such as a monitor, as used in a color management system.

Color Rendering Dictionary (CRD) - The output profile used by a PostScript printer. This is a lookup table used to define how colors are produced on a printing device.

Compression - Algorithms used to reduce the size of computer data files. Widely used to reduce very large graphic files.

Continuous Tone Images (CT) - Images that are represented by a range of colors or shades of gray and called continuous tone images. These images may be artwork or photographs, and can be represented in color or grayscale. Continuous tone images have not been screened.

Contrast - The difference in brightness between the lightest and darkest tones in an image.

Creep - When the inner-most pages of a signature are pushed outwards due to stacking of the pages in the signature.

Crop - The function of reducing the size of an image by permanently discarding information on the perimeter of the image.

Descreening - A method of removing or eliminating moiré patterns from an image when scanning.

Desktop Publishing (DTP) - Desktop publishing software is any application program that allows you to arrange text and graphics to create a document. Generally this term refers to high-end software programs.

Digital Front End (DFE) - See RIP

Dithering - The technique of using patterns of dots or pixels to create the effect of an intermediate tonal value.

Dmax - The Maximum Density in an image. See Shadow Point

Dmin - The Minimum Density in an image. See White Point

Dot Gain - The result of ink/toner spread and absorption into the paper during printing. Results in darker tones, especially midtones.

DPI - Dots Per Inch. A measure of the output printing resolution of laser printers and imagesetters.

Duplex - (Perfecting) Printing on both sides of a page.

EPS - Encapsulated PostScript. A subset of the PostScript page description language used to define a single page of artwork, which can be placed into an EPS compatible application.

Fonts - Any representation of alphanumeric information in a document. There are hundreds of various font styles available for use. The two most common font types are PostScript Type 1 and TrueType.

Gamma Correction - The measure of contrast that results in the lightening or darkening of the midtone regions of a document.

Grayscale - A continuous tone image made up of a number of shades of gray.

GCR / UCR - Gray component replacement / under color removal - methods of replacing combinations of cyan, magenta, and yellow with black, while retaining the visual representation of the colors.

Gutter Margin - The blank space, or inner margin from the printing area to the binding.

Halftone - A technique of converting a continuous tone image into dots, representing the individual tones of the image.

Halftone Cell - A cluster of individual printer dots. These dot clusters of color trick our eyes into perceiving distinct shades.

Halftone Screen - A halftone screen is the representation of a continuous tone image divided into a grid pattern and used in printing that image. This is an out dated term related to how screens (glass plates with lines etched horizontally and vertically) were used to convert continuous tone images into printing plates using a photographic process.

Highlight - The lightest desirable tone in an image, above which all tones are rendered as pure white.

HSB/HSL - Colors are defined by Hue, Saturation, and Brightness/Lightness.

Hue - The wavelength of light that represents a color. Hue is the most differentiating attribute of a color.

ICC Profile - A file that contains the mathematical color characteristics of a device (i.e. scanner, printer, monitor) in a color workflow. ICC profiles are used in conjunction with some color management systems.

Imagesetter - A device used to rasterize data and create printing plates for the offset printing process.

Imposition - The positioning of pages on a signature so that after printing, folding, and cutting, all pages will appear in the proper sequence. This term is also sometimes used to describe printing multiples of the same image on a sheet of paper.

Jaggies - See aliasing

Lamination - Lamination is the application of a thin plastic film to a document. This film adds durability to the document and is common on book covers.

Line Art - Any graphic image that is not a halftone image. Line art may be composed of one or more colors.

Lossless - A method of compressing graphic image data that does not degrade image quality.

Lossy - A method of compressing graphic image data by eliminating some redundant information. Results in loss of image quality.

LPI - Lines Per Inch. The measure of the frequency of halftone screen images in the printing process. Refers to the outdated method of using screen etchings to create halftones.

Lookup Table (LUT) - A reference file used to convert images from one colorspace to another. LUTs define the relationship between two data sets. Example: a table used to convert RGB data into CMYK for printing.

Midtone - The range of tones in an image located approximately halfway between highlights and shadows.

Moiré - An undesirable pattern created when printing with misaligned halftone screen angles. May also be created when scanning previously halftoned images.

Mottle - Mottling is uneven spotty toner coverage which occurs when printing large, solid areas of flat color. Paper choice can be critical in avoiding this problem.

Offset Lithography - A printing process utilizing liquid ink and printing plates to create an image.

PDF - Portable document format file type developed by Adobe Systems. This file type was designed to improve document portability because it is cross platform compatible and printer independent. The PDF format is becoming more acceptable in the commercial printing industry.

PDL - Page Description Language.

Perceptual (Photographic) - Used for photographic images. The intent is to preserve the visual relationship between colors in a way that is perceived as natural to the human eye. Single colors may not be reproduced exactly to maintain relationships between colors.

Pixel - The individual elements used to represent an image on a computer monitor.

PostScript - A general-purpose page description language used to represent computerized image data in the printing industry. PostScript is considered the standard language of the commercial printing industry.

PPD - PostScript Printer Description, a special file used to define the output options for a specific printing device. PPDs are used by some Windows based applications and by Macintosh computers to define printing devices.

PPI - Pixels Per Inch. The representation of the number of pixels used to create an image on a computer monitor.

Print Driver - A piece of software used to control or "drive" a peripheral device such as a scanner or printer.

Print Ready File - A computer file that has been converted into a PostScript language file and is ready to be submitted to a RIP for printing. Print ready files will contain all information, fonts and graphics, necessary for printing.

Print To File - The process of converting an application file into a print ready file using a specific printer driver.

Process Color - The CMYK primary colors used in process color printing.

Profile/Device Profile - The description of a device's color gamut. It is a type of lookup table that describes the device-dependent color gamut of the printer or scanner in relation to a device-independent CIE model.

Quarter Tones - The tones in an image that lie between the midtones and the highlights. Three quarter tones lie between the midtones and the shadows.

Raster - See Bitmap.

Reflow - Reflow affects the character spacing within fonts and adds more space than was intended. Reflow can change the layout of the entire document. Reflow can occur when one element of the original file is missing in the file that you give to your service provider. Providing an accurate hard copy proof with your digital files will allow this error to be caught and corrected.

Relative Colorimetric - Used for printing company logos and where a specific color must be reproduced as exactly as possible. This intent compares the white point (extreme highlight) of the source colorspace to that of the destination colorspace, and shifts all colors accordingly. Colors that cannot be reproduced are reproduced as closely as possible.

RGB - Red, Green, Blue, the additive primary colors used to display data on a computer monitor.

Rendering intent - Settings used to define how RGB colors will be converted to a CMYK gamut. There are four different types of rendering styles used for different types of documents. The four types are typically called:

Absolute Colorimetric
Relative Colorimetric
Perceptual
Saturation

Resample - To change the resolution and resulting size of an image by removing or adding of data in the file.

RIP - Raster Image Processor. A computer device that converts data into a bit mapped image used in the printing process.

Saturation (Presentation) - Used for business graphics. The intent is to preserve the vividness of the color rather than the accuracy of the color. This intent scales the source gamut to the destination gamut but preserves the relative saturation instead of the hue.

Saturation - The amount of gray in a color. Less gray results in more saturation.

Shadow Point - The samples in an image that will print in the darkest tone possible for a specific output device. Tonal values below this point will print as pure black.

Sharpening - A technique of increasing the contrast between all ranges of the tonal difference within an image.

SPI - Samples Per Inch. A measure of the number of data points per inch that a scanner captures.

Spot Colors - Inks created to conform to a specific spot color system. They are generally used to enhance a four-color process job or when the print job does not require full color images and less than four colors will meet the customers needs.

Subtractive Color - This is the method used to create all printed materials. The subtractive primaries are cyan, magenta, yellow (CMY). Subtractive colors are created when light reflecting off the printed surface, part of the light is absorbed by the surface (subtracted) and we see the remaining portion of the light.

SWOP - Specifications for web offset publications - a set of standards for offset printing that contain specifications for ink, paper, print densities, etc.

TIF - Tagged image format graphic image file type. The TIF image is a cross platform file type compatible with most application programs.

Trapping - Trapping is a technique in which adjacent colors slightly overprint each other to help minimize the affects of possible misregistration.

TrueType Fonts - A computerized font type used to represent alphanumeric information in documents. TrueType fonts are common to both Windows and Macintosh computer platforms.

Type 1 Fonts - A computerized font type used to represent alphanumeric information in documents. Developed by Adobe Systems and are considered the standard for the printing industry.

Unsharp Masking - A technique of increasing the contrast at border areas of significant tonal difference within an image.

White Point - The samples in an image that will print the lightest tone possible of the intended output device.